The Outline of our Souls

The Outline of our Souls:

Unitarian Universalist Church of Davis Worship Associate Reflections

Contents

Contents

Contents

Contents

Editorial Team

This project was pieced together with the vision, time, and talents of this editorial dream team:

Susan Steinbach
Mary Higgins MacDonnell
Karen Klussendorf Kurth
Lorraine Nail Visher
Catlyn LeGault

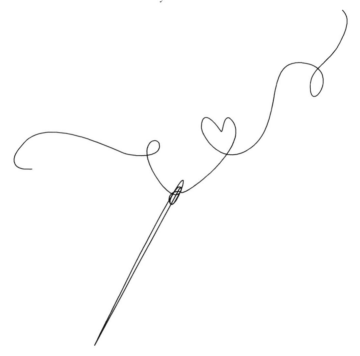

Illustrations were created by Catlyn LeGault and were inspired by these writings and the Unitarian Universalist Church of Davis as a whole.

Introduction

Writing can operate as alchemy, transforming thoughts and feelings from mere whispers into full thought, passion and meaning. Written words give shape and substance to poetry and reflection. They challenge us with a path of discovery and call us to account for our actions. Writing is both a risk and a reward.

When the writing process is supported and given shape within the shared ministry of a spiritual community, it can become truly magical. Such is the legacy of the Unitarian Universalist Church of Davis, California (UUCD). The Rev. Beth Banks fostered our Worship Associate program during her 22 year tenure as our Senior Minister.

The responsibility of a Worship Associate is to reflect on and study the deeper questions and meaning of a given worship service. Each associate brings the fullness of this study, mixes it with their own understanding of life, and heats it in the crucible of writing. The palpable result, shared orally during the service, may elicit a nod of the head, a soft murmur, a brief chuckle, or even a tear.

In 2007 the first collection of such reflections entitled *In this Quiet Light* was assembled and published under the editorial leadership of congregants/writers Ruth Hall, Ann Halsted, and Ray Coppock.

Now in 2024, UUCD moves into a different chapter by welcoming our newly-called Minister, the Reverend Angeline Jackson. In *The Outline of Our Souls*, we as a congregation pause and look back at the wisdom, insight and compassion of our Worship Associates over the years since 2007 leading us to this momentous transition. We wonder, what might Rev. Angeline prompt our congregation to co-create with her in the years ahead?

Gentle reader, we invite you to settle in and enjoy these reflections, whether for the first time or as a fond reprisal, savoring the gifts of services past, prompting your own journeys of the spirit, heart and soul.

Susan Steinbach & Lorraine Visher
Co-Editors

This is You
Lorraine Nail Visher

If you feel discouraged
write about your despair.
If you think it's stupid
write it anyway.

If you write it and hate it
you have the power
to laugh about it,
cry about it,
rewrite it
or
throw it away!

The important thing is
to keep your pen,
or pencil,
moving across the page.
Write this word, then the next
and the one after that.
Even if they don't fit together.
Write until your hand hurts.
Then stop.

Look at it again
another day.
you might find what you thought
was prose
is hiding a poem.
What you thought was a poem
becomes a story and a story
becomes a song.

If no voice is speaking
make up a voice.
Lie, mimic, pretend, preach.
The important thing is not to wait
for the muse.
You *are* the muse.

Say too much or don't say
enough.
Write 3 words or 3000.
Leave the damn page blank
for weeks, months,
but please,
not years.

There is no purpose to this.
There is no standard or command
that you cannot shove aside.

This is you,
creating the outline
of your own soul.

In the Company of Others
By: Carlena Wike

Standing on this side of the podium now that I am, by virtue of my years, a bona fide elder, I am aware of a shift in perspective. I used to think of time as linear; but these days, time seems malleable. I have become my own grandmother, handing memories out like chiclets to anyone who will listen.

I remember being a Worship Associate for a couple of Milton Hildebrand's annual summer sermons. Milton was a frequent and celebrated speaker in the early days of the fellowship and when he spoke, you could be certain to spot a clutch of our founders in the sanctuary. Their enthusiasm was palpable and I was struck by a moment of clarity— that I was in community with the people who dreamed and sweated this space into being added dimension to my experience. I came to equate the expansion of this church with the growth of the trees around it planted by those who laid the foundation, raised the walls and opened the doors to welcome the future in.

Although most of the founders are available in the archive of memories shared, I am aware of a spiritual reciprocity going on here, especially when granted a pulpit view of the congregation

It's a bit like examining a cross-section of a redwood tree and considering the history represented in each of its rings. Everyone who has joined and nurtured the community has added to that history and those who have left us remain a part of it.

I am aware of my history here, that I am, in some small way, included in the outer twenty rings. I am deeply grateful for having had the privilege of being in community with many of the people who dreamed the dream and planted the seed that grew into the church whose beauty and shelter we now enjoy.

As we add our joyful noise today to this history, let us honor the past, work in the present and build toward a shared vision for the future.

Chalice Lighting

When we gather and ignite this flame
something is born of us
and in the hush which follows
we feel one more presence
than was counted crossing the threshold—

For, so gathered, we create a body for this church
and each of us, in the company of others,
provides the living breath and beating heart
of a being bent toward goodness.
We offer and receive its sanctuary—
Hold out and are held in its arms—
And when we leave, we do not leave alone.

Gratitude and Arrival
By: Kirk Ridgeway

March 2, 1997. I am flying home from Florida after yet another visit to my parents, both with serious life-limiting illnesses. Alone and deep in thought, I think about their impending deaths.

The pilot's voice fills the cabin, *"Ladies and Gentlemen, this is your Captain speaking. We have a warning light indicating that our landing gears may not be fully down and locked. We are going to fly by the control tower so they can have a look. This is a precautionary measure as we believe that the wheels are fully extended. Please do not be alarmed."*

We fly by the tower. The flight attendants become very focused and professional. *"Ladies and Gentlemen, this is your Captain speaking. The wheels seem to be okay and we will be landing in a few minutes. As a precaution, flight attendants, prepare the passengers for an emergency landing."* This is no joke, no drill, this is the real thing. All the passengers are amazingly quiet except for a few whispered conversations and soft sobs. The flight attendants instruct us to remove everything from our pockets and all jewelry.

I withdraw into my world. Rationally assess the realities of my situation. Imagine the plane breaking up, how I will escape if I survive the impact, how smoke and fire will certainly consume the cabin and probably me. Prepared to fight for my life, I prepare to die. I begin saying goodbye...naming one-by-one my closest friends, then my parents and sisters, then my children.

We circle and approach the airport for a second time to land. We assume the braced impact position. In loud directive voices the flight attendants chant, *"Bend Over! Heads Down! Stay Down!" "Bend Over! Heads Down! Stay Down!"* Their chant is strangely calming. In this calmness, I say goodbye to the great love of my life, my wife Linda. With the wheels about to hit the runway the chant intensifies, changes to, *"Heads Down! Heads Down! Heads Down!"* My head on my knees, my hands wrapped around my ankles, I continued to whisper, *"Goodbye Linda. I love you. Goodbye Linda. I love you. Goodbye. Goodbye. Goodbye."*

The wheels hold. No smoke, no fire. What fills the passenger cabin is resplendent joy. Cheers and applause erupt for the Captain and the crew as the fire trucks and ambulances withdraw. We rejoice with boundless gratitude and the unspoken understanding of the intimate relationship we all shared together, as one, in these moments.

There are many teaching points in our lives, some indelible. This was one of them. All the trappings of my life were stripped away on that sharp edge of death. A crystalline clarity emerged to reveal the essence of my life. If I had any questions about what I valued, how I valued, and how I wanted to claim my happiness, it was eradicated in those moments. And what I choose to love is happiness born of gratitude grown in the garden of my most intimate relationships.

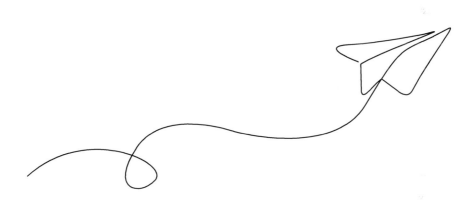

Mud Shoes and Drip Cathedrals
By: Lorraine Nail Visher

Water rites and rituals exist in every religion usually representing purification. Baptism uses submersion in water, Moses parted the waters, the dead are cleansed with water, as are young adults as a rite of passage. Water can represent a great journey or remind us of the impermanence of life. Each of us has our own personal relationship with water. Here is a bit of mine.

I grew up on a farm. A ranch actually. Farms evoke images of row crops and farm animals. A ranch denotes cattle or orchards. Mine was the later. Although the Sacramento and San Joaquin rivers converged a mere ten miles away, the ground my grandfather worked was dry and fiercely divided between sifting sand and petrified clay. Water was seduced into being each summer with smooth concrete canals to slide upon, tall standing pipes in which to fly and pressurized well casings which occasionally overflowed and exploded into fountains. From a rattling trailer behind the tractor, long metal pipes were painstakingly laid-out section-by-section between the almond trees. Today, the ka-chick, ka-chick, ka-chick sound of sprinkler heads heralds the coming of summer irrigation, but when I was a child the sound was a hiss. Each pipe section was pierced with small holes that spouted streams of pressurized water into the air where it vaporized into mist that spread between the trees.

My siblings and I regarded water as an elusive playmate. With water blasting from a garden hose we would drill to China until the sand collapsed inward and the hose became imprisoned like a downward snake. My father would find the tail still attached to a running spigot, swear, turn it off and slice off the hose at ground level. I'm sure the land is still riddled with rubber snakes standing on their heads.

The clay soil was more challenging, but a hose left running long enough could carve a delta through it. Streams diverged and created both canyons and wide swamps that we crouched beside and built cites of mud, drip by slow drip. Short, squat houses were watched over by gothic cathedrals and we competed to see who could trickle out the tallest, thinnest spire.

But the irrigation pipes were the greatest treasure of all. When we heard the splutter and hiss of water running through them we raced outside to balance on metal tightropes. We tried to capture the water by covering the holes with our toes but water won, escaping between the spaces and tickling the soles of our feet. Gradually, a cold slurry of mud formed around the pipes; we stalked through it, alternated with hot, dry sand, and created mud shoes, which we proudly marched back to the house … and across the kitchen floor.

Today we wouldn't think of leaving a hose running indefinitely purely for the enjoyment of small children. We've designed water efficient irrigation that dribbles slowly and directly into the soil and roots without ever appearing on the surface. As Climate Change disturbs our world, it's critical that we treat water as the precious substance it is. The unlimited freedom to explore and play with this magical element may not be available to future generations and I believe that is a serious loss.

Water was holy and carefully tended by my grandfather with shovel and pipe. Water built drip mud cathedrals and laid a shimmering green veil across the land. We were baptized in the orchards, first with blossoms, and then - with water.

Although I had been a UU for almost a decade, I gave myself
the space to explore topics that were just outside my
consciousness. I started a multi-year habit of writing and
continued to seek topics that exhume memory, that are filled
with physicality, and that help me know more about myself.

Stacie Hartung Frerichs

Say Yes to Life
By: Elli Norris

Each morning when I'm up and dressed and the bed is made, I do my morning ritual. I go to the bureau in my bedroom—my altar, really. On it are special mementos that call people and events to mind. I light a candle and say some words. Here are some of them:

> I give thanks for this New Day
> And I say
> Yes to Life.

"Yes TO LIFE." Why do I say that?

I **really** heard those words for the first time—I mean really **HEARD** them-- in a sermon at Trinity Methodist Church in Berkeley, where I was a member in the 1980s. Our church was deciding whether to become a Reconciling Congregation, welcoming all people no matter their sexual orientation, and the day before the vote our pastor, Ron Parker, based his sermon on these words that Moses said to his followers millennia ago:

> "…I set before you life and death, blessing and curse;
> therefore choose life that your descendants may live…"
>> Deuteronomy 30:19

That sounds pretty momentous. Huge! And for Moses and his people, that choice WAS huge. Not just for biological life, but for all qualities that make us human. Spiritual, ethical, psychological.

Ron made clear that we all make important decisions in our own lives, and that it's not always easy to choose which is the choice for life. What about a woman with several children who finds herself with an unplanned pregnancy? To have an abortion or not? What about the gay man deciding whether to come out at work or not? Risk his job or remain silent?

Now, I had discussed with Ron that I was lesbian and had lived in the closet all my life. I had grown up in conservative San Joaquin Valley, in a conservative family, and had chosen to come out to only close friends. But now, as our church faced a choice of becoming open to all gay and lesbian people, was I going to remain silent? Was it time to come out, now, in my 50s, to this whole congregation? Oh My God!

Fortunately, I realized that to remain silent would indeed be a choice for "death." I came out and people surrounded me with love. The church did vote to become a Reconciling Congregation—not because I had come out, but because it was the right time to do it. For me, my choice was the beginning of another, freer chapter in my life.

I'm telling you this story this morning not as yet another "coming out" story. I'm telling it because this is my pearl for you: "Say Yes to Life." It has become my mantra, and it raises my spirits when I remember to say it, even when the decision doesn't seem very important.

For example, this morning my feet hurt and my knees ache so I feel a little wobbly on my feet. What shall I do? Stagger onward with sore feet and no cane; carry a cane and gripe about it all day, or just laugh at vanity and carry my cane with a swagger.

And this YES to Life, Life As It Is, lifts my spirits. I hope I will be able to say Yes when I am faced with more critical decisions.

No, I don't always say Yes, or even remember to Say Yes to Life to start my day.

But when I do remember, my day goes better.

Career Mothering
By: Karen Klussendorf Kurth

Mother's Day 2023

The only job I truly and deeply wanted was to be a Mother.

Starting at age eight, I babysat the neighborhood toddlers and babies – trading for a quarter per hour or piano lessons, always accompanied by refrigerator access. Babysitting continued through my teen years and started to include making dinner, light cleaning with maybe fifty cents an hour (still accompanied by refrigerator access). At age 14 I had a "second family" with a one and three-year-old with whom I spent most of my free time. They invited me to live in Australia with them for part a of year as a live-in nanny. A solid yes.

Upon returning home to Wisconsin, Pop died and I absorbed many of the family duties while Mom worked. As a single working mother with four teens, she didn't have much choice but to let us raise ourselves the rest of the way. More parenting practice – while I continued babysitting and working in the church's childcare.

By the time high school came, it was no secret that I wanted my own kids. Ever the over-planner, I told my peers I'd most likely have kids first (and a jeep) and then see if a marriageable person came along who would fit into my family. My plan was sincere.

As it turns out, I went a more traditional route and married when I was 22, with the promise that we'd wait until I graduated from college to have kids.

19

Three years later I finished school and became pregnant the month after graduation. With all my experience I pretty much knew what I was getting into and felt ready and prepared.

There was a prepared childbirth class where parents-to-be shared upcoming concerns and fears. Most feared the pain of childbirth, of not getting enough sleep or dropping the baby. My response "That will be over in no time, I'm more concerned about the next 25 years!" was met with stunned expressions. It was as if the young parents hadn't considered the lifelong commitment they were making.

In the 80's it was typical to be asked "Why would you bring kids into THIS world?" – to which I would confidently answer, "MY kids are going to make this world better." Yes, I proceeded to have a strategically planned and amazing daughter and son.

Parenting has been both the easiest and hardest responsibility I've had… and continue to have. My greatest joys and pains, confidence and concerns, pride and confusions have all come with parenting. I've had other deeply satisfying and challenging jobs – but none that match parenting, which has indeed been the challenge I expected. It is also true that my kids *have* made this world a better place.

Regardless how prepared or ready one may be – parenting is hard. Certainly, in being a parent over the last 40 years, I've cultivated more insight and compassion towards my own parents. I believe they mostly did the best they could do and when they didn't do their best, I believe they earned a lot of latitude. After all, how does one set out to "raise" someone with confidence, compassion, adventure and independence when you may have thought keeping them alive was the only requirement? (We can't all send our fourteen-year-old daughters half way around the world with a second family.) My mother certainly never failed at parenting (though I surely told her so)! In fact, I'd say she did quite well, and I believe I've done pretty darn well myself.

As I embark upon a new adventure called grandma-hood, I find myself ill-prepared. Grandparenting will be more spontaneous and I'll have to embrace my mis-steps. There is a dawning realization that there will be endless "firsts", there will be joys to outnumber the heartbreaks, and that this is a lifelong career. Regardless of my confidence as a young parent, becoming a grandma comes with uncharted adventure and with a whole lot of new rules. My expertise will get me nowhere as I witness my son becoming a father and follow the lead he and his wife lay out. They are the parents now.

It is absolutely true that being a Mom has been my greatest challenge, my greatest adventure, and... my deep honor. As it turns out it was a good career choice, and in the choosing, I *have* made the world a better place. It is now my great honor to navigate my new role as Grandma K. I have much to learn and beg much latitude.

Happy Mother's Day!

May the Source Be With You
By: Ben Bazor

I'm sure this or something like it has happened to many of you.

Up in the morning. There isn't any coffee around. Tired. Get in the car and go into reverse and thud. [*Sigh*] Bumped into a car. Left a scratch. Dang....

Then the thoughts appear. Like the demon and angel advising us from our shoulders, one voice says, "Come on, no was hurt, no one saw. And please, look at their car, there are already so many scratches. You couldn't even tell." Then the other voice comes, "Ben, you know what the right thing to do is. Do it. Leave a note."

The light side and the dark side. I'm sure each voice has won out sometime or another for all of us. That day, for me, the dark side won. I scratched a car and just sorta left. [Grimmace]

Still I try to be a good person. I'd like to believe that I'd make a decent jedi. But today isn't about the consistency of my moral character or my fugitive status from a minor traffic accident. It is about the question of where does the good voice come from? Who or what guides your inner moral compass? By whose authority do you define right and wrong?

When I first pondered this question, one source instantly came to mind - my Dad. His words echo in my mind to this day, "Is that the right thing to do, Ben?" My dad would often say this in incredibly mundane situations. As a kid, making a mess in the grocery story, "Someone will have to clean that. Is that the right thing to do, Ben?" As a teen, parking sloppily and taking two spots, "Is that the right thing to do?"

Over time I started to internalize Dad's voice and the principles he was trying to teach -- be generous, be polite, don't inconvenience others and treat people the way you'd like to be treated.

Where else does that voice come from?

I didn't grow up UU (Unitarian Universalist), so I never specifically internalized the Seven Principles but while I grew up in a secular house, my parents were both raised Christian. They didn't pass on the dogmas, but as I've grown older, it's been clear that the moral teachings are engrained in them as they have been engrained in me. Forgiveness. Kindness. Patience. Knowing that things would be a lot different if you were walking in another's shoes.

These teachings -- implicit or explicit -- from my parents and the cultural context of my upbringing, were not comprehensive, but were rather individual examples that spoke to larger principles.

Now, I've never read the Bible, but I'm reasonably certain Jesus never said "Thou shalt smile at your checker in the grocery store." But I bet if you'd ask, he'd say, "Well yeah! Smile at people!"

This comes to the last source I've found - myself. The principles I was taught and agreed with became internalized. I'd try them out in different situations and they'd grow more nuanced with time and reflection on the complexity of life. If being generous is good, then my seven year old self thought giving my toy Millennium Falcon to my brother's friend would be good. He loved it, but my parents were sad when I parted with a gift they had given me. Generosity is more complicated than just giving everything away.

So next time you're in a moral struggle, I invite you to consider who is sitting on your shoulder?

Being a Worship Associate helped me explore my own theological beliefs and gave me the opportunity to share them with the whole congregation. This created a simpatico between us.

Lorraine Nail Visher

Valuing Women's Work: A Reflection on Families
By: Robin Datel

My reflection is about women and work in five generations of my maternal family. Let me make clear at the outset that our experiences have been shaped by the middle-class status of most of the family units in this story.

Lucky Detroit women in the late nineteenth century enjoyed beautiful clothes handmade by my great-grandmother Dora, a women's tailor. She gave up that work when she married my great-grandfather and raised not only the seven children she had with him, but also his two children from a previous marriage and at times, the children of her daughter Alice. Alice had died from a back-alley abortion, which she had chosen rather than expose another child to her abusive husband. By giving up paid employment in exchange for running a household and raising children, Dora left what is often called the productive labor force to join the reproductive one.

Reproductive labor does not refer solely to childbearing and rearing but to all types of activities that support the continued creation of the labor force needed by an economy. I want to draw to your attention two aspects of reproductive labor: that it is often performed by women and that it is often unwaged.

Dora's daughter Amy was my maternal grandmother. She had some secretarial training after completing the eighth grade and eventually went to work for the Hammond Lumber Company in Humboldt County. She married a manager in the same firm and after that became a homemaker and raised two children, one of whom was my mother, Dorie. World War II provided the opportunity for Amy to rejoin the productive labor force, and when her husband died shortly thereafter, she returned to work for the military.

My mother had one brief failed marriage, two years of college, some brief stints of paid employment (including as a Rosie the Riveter) before she married my dad. I consider her a super-worker in the reproductive labor force, not only raising two children, but contributing to the well-being, character formation, and education of girls through leadership in the Girl Scout movement. She returned to the paid labor force thirty years after leaving it, having completed undergraduate and master's degrees, as a research librarian at Western Costume Company in Hollywood. Her love of clothing and textiles came from her grandmother, the women's tailor. I am moved by this intergenerational connection – that the productive work of my great-grandmother helped enable her granddaughter to find such a fascinating and creative job at age 53.

I had relatively little experience in the labor force until after I finished a PhD; then I worked first as a part-time faculty member and later obtained a full-time academic position. I am grateful to have had paid work that could to some extent expand and contract along with the changes in my family circumstances, which included at different times raising children and caring for my husband who had Parkinson's.

My younger son and his wife comprise the fifth-generation family in this narrative. My son has a chronic medical condition, which led him to leave the labor force, both to reduce stress, which aggravates his condition, and to protect him from COVID, as his treatment suppresses his immune system. My daughter-in-law, a computer scientist, is thus the productive worker in their household, while he has taken on more of the reproductive work.

Sketching some of the productive and reproductive work histories of women in my family reveals that options for the former have multiplied many times over. And this, in turn, has offered families more ways to arrange their lives together, creating more possibilities for happiness. Still, women continue to do the bulk of our country's reproductive labor, many without receiving wages in return, with implications for power dynamics and well-being within and beyond families.

So as UUs, let us not only continue to fight gender discrimination at work and at home, but also advocate for universal health care and universal basic income, which would be particularly supportive of reproductive workers and their families. Helping to secure these programs would activate our commitment to families – their holiness and wholeness - and give added meaning to the "Universalism" in Unitarian Universalism.

Relationships that Sustain Us
By: Mary Higgins MacDonnell

The phone rings, I say "Hello." I hear, "It's your sister." The voice on the other end sounds remarkably like my own voice.

I am the second born of three children in my family. I have a sister two years older than myself and a brother eight years younger. Growing up, I admired and sometimes emulated my older sister and often competed with her. I desperately wanted her approval.

When people asked me if my sister and I are close, I would sometimes pause and think, "Hmmm, is this what closeness looks like?"

One of my challenges growing up was that I feared my older sister did not like me. Now that I say it out loud, that's probably a very normal fear! We had different interests. My sister loved to read. I don't have any clear memories of her playing as a child. I was all about running, biking, jump rope and games. I remember begging her to play dolls with me, to no avail. When she got married, I was her one attendant. When I got married, she was my one attendant.

We never strayed too far from each other, but was it closeness? I looked for a certain style of support from her: to listen to my stories without interrupting and to offer less advice. That's what acceptance would feel like in my estimation.

In my 20's and 30's, I cultivated wonderful friendships with women who listened to me at length without interrupting and rarely offered advice. I felt accepted in these friendships. These were my chosen sisters.

Then my sister and her husband had a baby. They asked me to be the godmother. It was clear that my sister wanted me to be very involved in my niece's life. For the next four years I babysat, had my niece over for playdates, joined them for important milestones and generally shared the joy of a growing child. When they had their second daughter, I was well established as Aunt Mary, and now had two little ones to care for.

This is what a typical play date looked like. When my nieces arrived, they raced into my arms and locked a tight hug around my neck. I was unprepared for the unguarded love and affection my young nieces showered on me. We would pull the toy box out of the closet. This contained odds and ends for dress up, several toy trucks, dolls, etc. We usually got our hands dirty with a craft, such as making play dough from corn starch or creating hand puppets from athletic socks. Part of the magic was that we had unstructured time together to move at their pace. One of the ways my sister demonstrated her love was to give me a special role in the lives of her children.

My relationship with my sister has served as a lifelong teacher, about how to recognize love being offered. The fact is, my sister accepts me and wants the very best for me. My sister's caring has a constancy, it is always there for me. This is something which I could never have imagined nor created on my own. It feels sustaining, like the warmth of the sun.

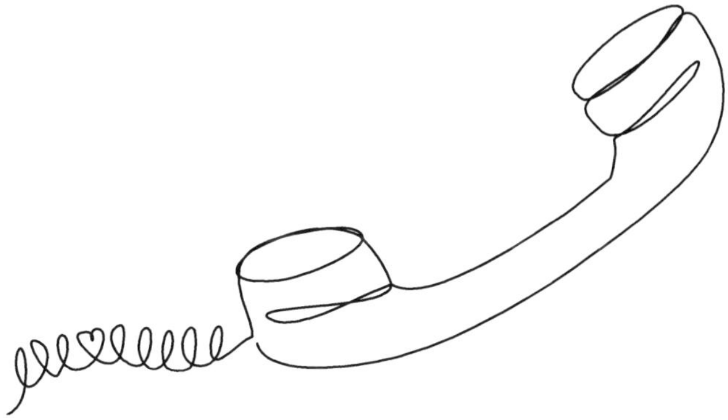

How Unitarian Universalism's Six Sources are Performing in the Climate Crisis
By: Robin Datel

When I was in elementary school in Eureka, California, my family (mom, dad, sister, and I) lived in a new mid-century modern home on the edge of town surrounded by redwood trees and huge hollow stumps that were left behind by logging. Lots of redwood went into that house, including the siding, the decking, the fencing, and a particularly large, beautiful slab of wood that formed the mantelpiece. This was no surprise, given that my Uncle Frank worked for the Arcata Redwood Lumber Company and that years before, my maternal grandfather was the sales manager for the Hammond Lumber Company, sometimes working in the company town of Samoa in Humboldt County and at other times at headquarters in San Francisco.

My maternal grandmother went to work for Alameda Naval Air Station after my grandfather, the redwood sales manager, died, making her part of our military-industrial complex with its high degree of dependency on, and entanglement with, fossil fuels.

My paternal grandparents were farmers in South Dakota. They experienced the transition from mixed farming to specialized monocultural wheat and corn cultivation, accompanied by a growing dependency on fossil fuel inputs in all phases of production.

My dad spent his entire career (1947-1986) helping to build the once-upon-a-time greatly admired California state highway system, including federal interstate freeways. He began as a junior civil engineer surveying the rough country of the Trinity River to improve Highway 299 and ended up as the California State Highway Engineer at Caltrans headquarters in Sacramento, with stops in various districts along the way.

I share with you these details of my family history to let you know how close I am to ways of making a living that were highly extractive, often unsustainable, often heavily polluting, and contributory to the climate crisis we face today. In addition to their environmental downsides, what my family members did for a living often disproportionately harmed BIPOC communities.

This is a painful admission. Sharing this information, I feel anxiety about fingering my parents and grandparents, whom I loved and admired. I personalize my message today not to single them out as culprits, but to illustrate how close to the bone are ways of life that we now must reckon with and radically reform in order that diverse others, human and otherwise, can survive and thrive.

I personally must make major changes to the way my parents and grandparents and my younger self lived. It is also up to me—and to us—to pressure our governments and our economies to make major changes. Otherwise, the terrible outcomes predicted by science—starvation, thirst, disease, displacement, death, extinction—of humans, plants, animals, entire ecosystems—will come to pass. Minimizing that loss and suffering is my goal in revealing to you what I now recognize as the accumulated debts of my family—and millions like them—living middle-class lives in mid-twentieth-century America.

Recently I shared with you a message about the climate crisis and imagination. I advocated that you read Kim Stanley Robinson's cli-fi novels *New York 2140* and *The Ministry for the Future* because he is able to imagine a future ravaged by the climate emergency but with room for humans to push back with creativity and efficacy.

I urge you to draw on the sources of our living tradition as we imagine the future. I use the sources to paint a mental mural that depicts what I want to save and what I need to do. My mural includes . . .

- Images of speckled Sierra Nevada granite splashed by rambunctious white water, a California tidepool colorful and animated with life, and all of us—young and old and middle-aged together—singing with joy. (Inspired by the first source[1])

- Images of protest marches and vigils and sit-ins and public meetings and phonebanks and letters to the editor and donations given and poems written and impassioned speeches delivered and climate-friendly laws passed. (Inspired by the second source[2])

- Images of world religious leaders with thought bubbles featuring what is good in our astounding Creation. (Inspired by the third source[3])

- Images of people loving not only their diverse human neighbors, but also their plant and animal neighbors, as themselves. (Inspired by the fourth source[4])

- Images of natural and social scientists looking at the world through lenses of rational inquiry and with an air of love and humility. Behind them are depicted technologies and systems, many of which we have already figured out, that will help us leave fossil fuels in the ground and build a regenerative way of life. (Inspired by the fifth source[5])

- An image of the Tending and Gathering Garden* at the Cache Creek Nature Preserve, where Wintun culture bearers practice and teach traditional reciprocal ways of living with the land. (Inspired by the sixth source[6])

May we be inspired by these sources of our living tradition, and others— since we believe that revelation is not sealed—to embrace and work for the changes necessary to healing the many wounds that we, including those we love, have inflicted on Earth and her creatures.

I love writing but seem to need an assignment! I treasure the experience of having a topical assignment along with a gentle hand urging me to dig deep.

Karen Klussendorf Kurth

Nature Mystic
By: Karen Friis

The wheelbarrow is full of potting soil, earthworm castings, green sand and seed planting medium. The pots are clean and stacked. The basket is brimming with seed packets and the brightly-colored labels are itching to be placed in the pots. Looking out from the deck onto the meadow, the baby blue eyes, daffodils, tulips, buttercups, lush grasses, and bird song all invite us further into the joy of spring. I close my eyes and Spirit is surrounding me.

My women friends arrive, full of the hope and ecstatic anticipation of our day. This is our annual gathering for seeding our flowers and veggies for our gardens. We spread out all our seeds, excited to share our favorite new and tried-and-true finds.

My friend, Richard calls me a nature mystic…mmmm! That is a lovely image.

Moving from a traditional sense of faith, raised in the Methodist tradition, to this new spiritual practice has been a journey.

I am aware of how much I move with the seasons, listening, singing, and holding the Divine close. She is EVERYWHERE!

I hunker down in the darkness of winter, marveling at the trunks of the crepe myrtle, cuddling up under my quilt, listening to music and reading, being aware of the rain and the incessant wind of Davis. The darkness is punctuated by my candles and twinkly lights around my home.

And of course, there is singing in a circle, bundled up with blankets with my song sisters, which keeps me in touch with the simplicity of life, with the Divine, and the intimate love I feel for these amazing women in my life.

My midday walks in the greenbelt, being aware of the glistening grasses and barren beauty, keeps me sane. In my garden, broccoli, cauliflower, spinach, chard, and kale make my garden and my tummy happy while I watch the garlic bulbs pop their heads up as the warmth returns. "And the seasons, they go round and round".

Glorious spring planting, wildflower field trips to Capay Valley, I sing as I move through my day, no matter where I am. Then onto summer harvest, hours of putting up red and green salsas and jams with sister Stephanie and other friends, hiking in the cool of the Sierra, inhaling the "dessert" of the wildflower blooms yet again. Finally, I head into the autumn calm and the vibrancy of color splashing everywhere.

Mother Earth invites the Divine into my awareness, and singing calls-the Spirit into my heart and my body. Can you feel it? The cathedral of our beautiful planet is beckoning.

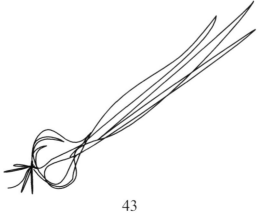

43

A Quiet Epiphany
By: Kirk Ridgeway

The hand moves
And the fire's swirling takes different shapes
All things change when we do
The first word, "Ah"
Blossoms into all others
Each of them is true.

In these words by the 1st century monk Kūkai, we can hear his experience of epiphany—an experience of amazing intensity that pierces the dark veil of consciousness to allow some bright light to shine through. A sudden shape-shifting realization of the heart and mind where something previously unknown or unseen is revealed. Its essence can be heard and felt in "The first word 'Ah' [that] blossoms into all others, each of them is true."

Epiphany is a BIG word which we usually associate with something grand, like the sky opening with a loud voice calling our name and we are bathed in a celestial shaft of light. Or an amazing dream waking us up on New Year's morning as a fully enlightened being, except for the hangover and the bags under our eyes.

There is another kind of epiphany. One that comes as a whisper. It arrives so softly that it can easily be missed if not listened for, looked for, longed for. This kind of quiet epiphany is the outcome of intentionality and attention.

Such was the case of an epiphany I experienced nineteen years ago on the small island of Iona off the rugged west coast of Scotland. How I arrived there is a very long story. Suffice to say, I was going through a time period often labeled as the "Dark Night of the Soul."

Alone, and intent on diving into the depths of my tumultuous interior landscape, I arrived cold, wet, and weary for it was a stormy North Atlantic day. A few days later I decided to walk the rocky perimeter of the island. It turned out be a physically challenging venture. The sky was dark, threatening, and wild.

As I walked, I wrestled with my stormy thoughts and feelings, asking and answering questions, then asking the questions again and again. Belongingness was the central theme.

Late in the day I arrived at a sheltered cove hungry, exhausted, and wet to the bone. Throughout the day I had experienced moments of ecstatic joy from seeing, hearing, feeling the raw power of the raging North Atlantic Ocean. And moments of knee-buckling grief as I played back memories and stared into a dark, frightening future.

Kneeling on that rocky beach, looking west across the immensity of the rough ocean towards home, I watched the clouds open and close across the face of the sun. In that moment I experienced a quiet epiphany. It whispered. I barely heard it above the waves. Some deep interior voice, call it the soul's voice. All the tensions of my body melted away.

In that moment I experienced a sudden intuitive realization of my absolute aloneness and my absolute belongingness...not only my belongingness to this world, but a vital belongingness to the Greater Story of everything there is. It was a cohesive soulful understanding of my inner and outer life.

This quiet epiphany is perhaps the greatest touchstone of my life - a moment I return to over and over both in my joys and in my sorrows. It was an intimate invitation to participate in the Great Dance. An invitation I could not, and will not, refuse.

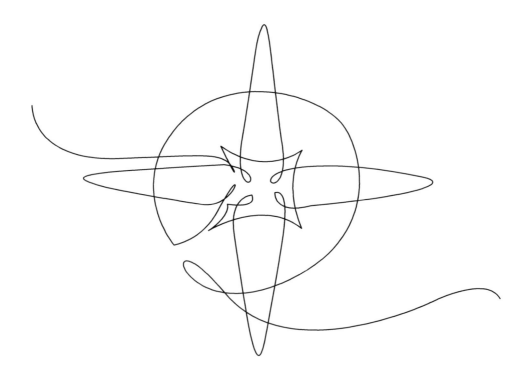

Cave Wisdom
By: Laura Sandage

My parents sought out caves. Our typical family vacation consisted of a loaded station wagon, a long drive, campsites, hikes, maybe some Indian ruins, and a cave tour. To be honest, most of the cave experiences blend together in my mind, creating a montage of cold air and handrails, stalactites and "cave bacon" formations, drippy "organ pipes" and murky underground streams, and the inevitable dramatic moment when the tour guide turns off the lights and asks us to try to look at our hands in the pitch blackness.

There is one family cave adventure I remember more specifically. It was the Lava Tube at Sunset Crater Volcano National Monument in Arizona. This cave was formed by cooling rivers of lava made of volcanic rock, not limestone. Our visit to the Lava Tube involved no tour guide, no handrails, and no electric lighting. We walked the barren landscape of the Lava Flow Trail visiting volcanic formations and trying our best to follow the somewhat ambiguous signs to the Lava Tube cave. We entered what we hoped was the Lava Tube on the assumption that we would crawl through an icy cold tube underground and come out the other end.

My six-foot four-inch dad led the expedition, with me, my little sister, and my mom following behind. Our weak flashlights did little to illuminate the situation as we crept through the narrowing passage, first crouching, then crawling, then slithering on our bellies, straining to make out the next bend in the path. When Daddy got himself wedged between two masses of stone on either side of his chest, we paused to assess the situation - it was a dead end. We would not come out the other side, but instead had to back up the train, slithering and scooting in reverse until we could turn ourselves around fully.

I think it was this moment of defeat that made the Lava Tube so memorable—a moment of reversal of fortune, of shifting perceptions. There were no fancy formations in the Lava Tube and no tour guide patter. Just a brave, hopeful family united in our determination to crawl through until suddenly we were a family that had been misled, a family on a fool's errand trying not to hit our heads and scrape our elbows as we retreated in chagrin and frustration. Were we wiser for the experience? I don't know. But it certainly was not a contemplative experience or a quiet gathering of inner resources that we found inside that cave.

In the dead end of the Lava Tube, we saw ourselves reflected: we saw our hasty assumptions, our hubris, our laughable stubbornness: dead ends all. We were forced to change our viewpoint, to reframe our assertions. If that is wisdom, then we were wiser. Emerging from the cold, dark cave, blinking our eyes in the heat and brightness of the Arizona summer, we resumed our family vacation and its pursuit of pleasure and adventure, peppered with moments of sibling animosity and marital discord to rival the Gods'.

I experience all the worship services differently [after being a Worship Associate]. I can see the act of creation happening each time.

Mary Higgins MacDonnell

Transitions
By: Ben Bazor

I've just traveled through one of the biggest transitions of a young person's life. Transitioning from my schooling to the workforce. I graduated from UC Davis about a year and a half ago. I started my current job full time nearly a year ago. I am very lucky to work in my field. But in that gap, I had no idea what the future would hold.

I had been in school in some form for the vast majority of my life - from the age of 4 to 22. Pretty much from the moment I stopped wearing a diaper, I was in a classroom. As the end of my schooling drew near, I was growing antsy. Once it arrived, the vacuum was a little unsettling. *How am I supposed to find the perfect career?* With great freedom, comes great anxiety.

The job search was daunting. I'd look on job sites and see countless listings for electrical engineers, mechanical engineers, civil engineers… A scant few for biomedical. Had I chosen the wrong major? Should I have interned with this or that company? The security blanket of education was off. I was left with my experiences and I had to find a way.

I connected with some folks at Shriners Hospital in Sacramento at the Motion Analysis Lab, where they put markers on the body to track limbs to make 3D computers models of moving bodies. While an undergrad, I had worked with the Shriners' team to create a device that aids in monitoring cerebral palsy. I asked if they needed help with anything. They offered part-time work.

The work was fun, but I knew it wasn't going to be my career. I had more income than I had in college for sure, but it was only enough to let me get by. What Shriners really gave me was time and peace.

Stripped of the anxiety of the job search, I had the opportunity to soul search. I could ponder:

* What do I want to do?

* Who do I want to be?

* How do I want to live?

* What are my goals?

I dreamed goals that were inspiring even if I didn't know how I would be able to achieve them. If I kept my eyes open, I trusted I could make them happen in the uncertain future. A small leap of faith.

Then I waited. I was contented to spend a year or so at Shriners before looking onward. Then after three months, I was hanging out with a friend from my major, whom I had only met because we sat together one day. He mentioned that he started to work for one of our old professors and they needed a biomedical engineer. He put in a good word for me and that is how I started to work with my current company.

I never expected to be where I am today. Looking back, my journey is clear. Yet my past self had no idea what the future had in store and there was no way it could have been planned out in advanced. The period of uncertainty had been bridged. In that time I grew tremendously, I had a crystallizing sense of clarity about who I was and achieved almost all the goals I had set at Shriners. One chapter has closed. Now the next chapter has begun.

A New Chapter Begins:
Reflection Written for the First Day of Transition Minister Rev. Connie Simon in the UUCD Pulpit
By: Susan Steinbach

Well, here we are. It's August 6, 2022. Our church has just said goodbye to two beloved ministers. Though we've known since last winter that they were retiring and transitioning, in the blink of an eye, those six months have flown by. We have feted them and honored their ministry with loving tributes.

Like many of you, I wiped away tears as Rev. Beth was presented with a quilt - one that was hand-stitched and signed by members of our congregation. Our connected web of touch blessed her and her quilt as our parting gift. *Well done, faithful servant…the mantle of parish ministry has been lifted. Let us sing Hallelujah.*

And now, they are gone.

I know I'm still personally grieving Rev. Beth Banks and Rev. Morgan McLean's absence, and perhaps some of you are too. I just can't quite get my head around the fact that we are to have no contact with them as they transition into their new lives, their new identities. But I'm working on it, I understand the reasons for it, and I'll get there in my head. We will have a new identity to forge for ourselves.

Look around the room, we are still here. The congregation is still here, well-established connections and relationships remain in place, even though many of our hearts are broken open. I would like to think we can move forward together and be open to change.

I've been a member long enough to remember the previous interim minister, Rev. David Keyes, who served between Rev. Jay Atkinson and Rev. Beth Banks in the late 1990s. Some of you might recall the first thing he told us was that we couldn't fire him – that he was temporary and he would be leaving when our next called minister was in place. And, he told us that we had a lot of work to do to get to that point....

I've been spending time processing my grief and inner unrest by doing what I always do, going out on the church grounds, watering, weeding, playing with my dog - something that is a routine and brings me comfort. While I am out there, I chew on the meaning of 'the church', 'the Davis church'.

What is the Davis Unitarian Universalist Church without Rev. Beth Banks or Rev. Morgan MacLean? They left their stamp on us, mentored us, ministered to us. What remains in our hearts and minds from their presence among us?

What was the church like before they came? It came to me slowly that they are NOT the church; they are one piece of a connected web that includes all of us, and to use Rev. Beth's words, *When one of us grieves a loss or celebrates a joy, the web of life bends and moves to a new shape.* We are the Church. What will our church be in 5 years, 15 years? How will we as a congregation take stock, grow, reinvent ourselves, attract newcomers, move forward?

Back to my story of seeking solace on the grounds last week, I look up from rewinding a garden hose, and I spy out across the parking lot what looks to be our new interim Minister, Rev. Connie Simon. She was moving items on a cart across the pavement into her new office. "Welcome! You're here!", I shouted. "So glad to meet you!" and likewise, she returned the same.

In that space between letting go and welcoming what's next lies the discomfort, the unknown, the reticence. But now, her smile was proof of a good plan that had come together – the Board and Interim search team have delivered to us a transition agent by the name of Rev. Connie Simon. And in the coming weeks and months, we are going to find out who she is and who we as a church can be together moving forward.

Bike Blessing
By: Donna Sachs

In my time at this church, I have always found it fascinating to learn how diverse we are in the ways we live our spirituality. A good opening to conversation is always, "What is your spiritual practice?" We share stories of transcendent experiences: of beauty, of meaning, nature, of deep love for others and for our world.

For me, practices that I have pursued teach me that the most precious spiritual reality of all is life as we are in it. In daily life, what we might call the mundane and the sacred merge into each other. Anything I do can become an expression of sacred connection. How I wash dishes. How I write a letter. How I bathe my granddaughter. How I grieve my mother. How I ride a bike.

Which brings me to today. Our bike-blessing day. I have been doing a certain bike-riding meditation that started years ago. I had read a report about an anthropologist who was meeting with first peoples in Australia, studying their myths and stories. One day, he was driving in the outback with a guide who was telling him stories of the dreamtime— specifically a story that involved the landscape they were traveling through. The guide kept talking faster and faster. Finally, our anthropologist asks, "Why are you telling this story so fast?" The guide responded, "Because we are driving so fast. The stories are for walking." The stories are meant to be walked. The lesson was, "Slow down!"

And then there was Orion, one of my favorite magazines. One feature present in each issue is called, "The Place where I Live." Readers are invited to send in short essays about where they lived. Back when I worked at the university, I would often commute by bike from my home, one-half mile out to the west of us, down the bike path along Russell to my office in the central UC Davis campus. It occurred to me that I could tell the story of the place where I live in the time it would take me to make my commute.

This spring, I have resurrected that project. And now, I have technology that I did not have then—a voice recorder app on my iPhone so I can read you a sample:

> I am on Russell Blvd, on the bike path that takes me home. I push off and ride leisurely along the avenue of the walnuts. I see the dead trees, the dying trees, the gone trees. Some stumps are four feet across. Back in the '80s, the canopy of these trees arched completely over the road. My daughter and I called it The Tunnel or The Dragon's Mouth. (As we drove: she would say, "Here we go—into the Dragon's Mouth!") The dragon's mouth is now wide open to the sky. On the left is a fence that looks out over university land. I see the lines of crops and orchards, and the signs of careful research being done. Someone's dissertation is out there.

> A yellow-billed magpie looks up at me from where he is pecking in the earth next to the asphalt. He is a creature who lives only here, in our area of Northern California. The wild mustard that grows all along our country roads and bike paths is taller than my head this year. Our winter rains were good for the mustard and for the rest of us. Out past Patwin Road now. On the north, groves of spindly trees have been removed and all is a neat agricultural area. Back in the '90s when those trees still existed, middle-school kids had built up hills for riding their dirt bikes.

I ride on past the Baptist church and to Cactus Corners, where the cacti have grown up taller than my head. Twice, in the years I have lived here, this cactus patch has frozen to the ground. First, in 1972—the first time I saw snow here in Davis. Second, in the bitter winter of 1989. Now they are once again resurrected.

The place where I live is holy ground. The place where we all live is holy ground. What a joy it is to experience it on a bicycle.

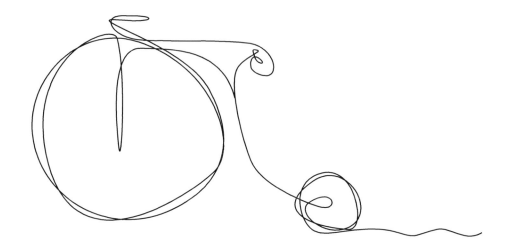

My Complicated Mother
By: Emily Burstein

My mom, Rose Ann Burstein, passed away in 2012 at age 89. She served as an impressive role model for me growing up in the 60s and 70s.

She received her first master's degree soon after WW II when both my parents attended graduate school and my mom also worked part-time to support them. Then a Masters in Library Science – earned at night when my brothers and I were young. She went on to be the head librarian at Sarah Lawrence College for over 20 years. At her memorial service, a number of the librarians recounted how she had been instrumental in supporting their careers, including helping them balance work and family.

My mother wasn't particularly bound by social mores. As adults we often visited my folks in Vermont, where in their late 50s, they built a passive solar summer home that was perched on top of a hill of rocky hay fields. On one visit with my two young sons we collected u-pick raspberries in the humid summer rain. My mom's pants became soaked below her knees. Without any hesitation, she took them off, wearing her rain jacket like a dress, to complete her berry picking. She was truly confounded when my husband was embarrassed.

Growing up, we explored countless neighborhoods in New York City: the garment district for material for sewing projects, the East Village to buy a pair of handmade leather sandals, and museums large and small. On these trips, we often searched out restaurants with non-European food, long before this was popular. Visiting the City, I became comfortable with a diversity of cultures and soaked up my parents' love of NYC in all its messiness and humanity.

Yet, when I think of my mom, my mind and heart often go to her cutting comments and the tension I'd feel deep in my body when we were together. Part of me was always guarded against the fear that her negative edge would jump out at any moment and cut me. She had an almost superstitious need to follow a positive comment with a negative one, to lead with a worry or negative reaction, poisoning any encouragement she might then offer me. Reading some old letters from my mom, I found that even now, some sentences make me feel like a deflating pricked balloon.

With time though, the sting of her voice has faded and I am no longer that deflated balloon. Instead, I find myself savoring her passion, strength, quirkiness, and trailblazing nature. My empathy bubbles up as I understand more and more about the wounding influences on her life. The Great Depression and her own negative and depressed mother impacted her deeply.

I have come to realize that I truly am a product of all my mother's parts. And that I get to choose which parts to nurture and which to let go. In so doing I honor her legacy and I tend to my own.

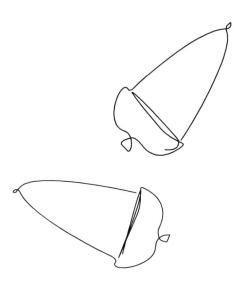

God as Prana
By: Karen Klussendorf Kurth

I found god.

I found a god I didn't know I was seeking nor imagined wanting. It turns out that my awkward concepts of 'god' had to do with vocabulary and naming. Theology, which I pictured as time consuming, cumbersome and unnecessary was not on my radar. Nonetheless, I ended up in a House for Hope adult RE theology class at the UU Church of Davis where indeed the readings felt 'churchy'.

I struggled with staying throughout the class, but I am not a quitter. If I sign up, I show up, so I considered how to make the most of it. I had to change course, open my mind and start the mindful practice of digging, questioning, and discerning. Though I never expected to realize a personal relationship with god, as I opened my heart in this search, I was getting personal. During a Word, Silence, Song meditation, it was as if a switch was thrown - I realized I did in fact know god. I had been simply unwilling to name it god.

I realized I find my god in Prana. Prana is the Sanskrit word for the life force that flows through everything and travels through the body on thousands of energy lines. Movement and breathing meditations make this energy sparkle for me. Mind, body and universe merge as time melts. Stillness and movement become one within a universal consciousness. God, with a capital G.

As I stood outdoors on a lovely Sunday in the rich landscape of our Davis church and tilted my forehead towards the sun, I experienced a synchronicity and merging with all living things. The spot between the eyebrows, the third eye, is considered the "Seat of Intuition, Creativity and the Deepest Personal Wisdom" in the Hindu and Buddhist traditions. As I exposed this spot to the sun, a life force engulfed me. I had felt this merging before and considered it merely a moment of reverence or relaxation. However, on that particular Sunday, it clicked together in a powerful way.

My God is Prana. I simultaneously wept and smiled with the familiarity of it all.

I've had rich, intuitive moments since my early years. My drive to connect has been evolving for a long time. In junior high I had to write a paper: "What I Believe" for Reverend Buffet, my Presbyterian youth pastor in Steven's Point, Wisconsin. I also had to sit with him and defend my paper – which boiled down to two pages of "I just don't know!". With great trepidation and a tight little sigh, I stepped into my appointment with Rev B and defended.

In the end, he nodded, looked *into* me and with a gentle smile and crinkly eyes he said, "You're on the right track, just keep going". His words stayed with me, but until now, forty years later, I didn't realize I have many more papers to write – and a new Rev B to sit with and assure me that "I'm on the right track, just keep going".

And so I continue the mindful practice of seeking, questioning and discerning as I lead with my heart and an open mind. I look for opportunities to feel the life force shake my soul and I see my God in the life force pulsing around me. I only need to reach out and keep going.

Being a Worship Associate has helped me spend significant time wrestling with very important issues and putting them into words in a reflection has helped crystalize how I feel about them. Helping lead worship services has helped me feel more a part of the fabric of the UUCD community.

Cliff Ohmart

Circling the Wagons: Living on the Side of Love
By: Autumn Labbe-Renault

It was after a high school football game that I cradled my friend Tony's head in my lap and tended to his black eye and the cuts on his cheek. Tony—and another friend, John—were the first male cheerleaders at our school. That night had been a home game, and as Tony walked to his car afterwards, a kid a year younger than us decided to take his fists to Tony's face. I found Tony a little later when I headed home. Slumped against a tire, he was a mess. Through his sobbing, I heard one word over and over – fag.

Tony had been beaten because he was gay. I wanted to get help—to call the police, to turn in the attacker. Tony wanted to let it go, telling me "It's not the first time, and it won't be the last."

I had led a pretty sheltered life. I didn't know that many gay people, but I had a few queer friends. People getting beaten up in parking lots, however, was outside my realm of experience. The horror of the AIDS crisis was unknown to me. All I knew was that my sweet, smart, funny friend was beaten because he was perceived as being different, and because the ways in which he was different threatened someone else's identity.

I worried after Tony and John the rest of that year. We never let them walk to their cars alone after that. We circled the wagons, so to speak. If Tony was unwilling or unable to pursue justice, then we'd make sure he didn't need to. I felt pretty proactive, pretty righteous.

And then I moved here to attend UC Davis, and like many a student before me, I became radicalized. Chiefly, that meant analyzing everything I knew through the lens of feminism. It would be another few years before I learned about Stonewall, or knew folks who were in Act Up, or attended a Pride festival. A few more until a good friend and a cousin came out. Even longer until I acknowledged my own bisexuality and had relationships with both women and men. Decades longer until I'd get to attend long-awaited civil unions and then weddings.

I think about Tony every June. I'm happy to tell you he's living his own "it gets better story". We reconnected a few years ago and he is married to a wonderful man, raising a daughter, and has a successful career. He was the first person who stirred in me awareness that people could want different things and love differently, and I'll always be grateful to him.

In my youthful zeal, I thought that getting angry and taking care of my friends was showing up for justice. My anger fueled my activism for years. It took me a long time to understand that anger burns out (and burns *us* out in the process), and that it takes a systemic overhaul of our beliefs and systems and institutions to effect real change.

Because I am happily married to a man, I recognize that I am afforded the privilege of being perceived as heterosexual. But identity is not the same as practice, and I do consider myself LGBTQ. My time in this church has taught me a great deal more about what it means to be welcoming, to be inclusive, to side with love—yours, mine, ours, Tony's, and anyone else who might need a good friend to show up in a parking lot on a really bad night. I will continue to live on the side of love.

Time Lines
By: Carlena Wike

I never know when epiphany will strike. This morning it hit as I hung the wash. Suddenly, the clothesline appeared to stretch the length of my life as though tethered to the T-shaped pole that held fresh sheets and towels on my mother's line in the mining camp of Monarch, Wyoming. The memories that cling to those lines still hold the perfume of laundry set out to dry in fresh air.

Suddenly my Rubbermaid laundry basket smelled like old wicker, the Delta Breeze became a Chinook, and I was hanging my father's cotton handkerchiefs, his balloon-bottomed boxers and his white starched shirts.

I was less than seven when I was allowed to help with the laundry as a diversion from running through it as it hung. I relished the responsibility of putting the clothes through the wringer into the rinse water, and then through it again into a wicker basket that I hauled in my wagon to the line. The lines were still quite a reach, but one had developed some slack and it became my training line, the place where I mastered the rules of hanging clothes.

Mother, who often seemed more feral than domestic, was unusually particular about laundry. One could not just pin things willy-nilly on the line. Mother taught clothes hanging as an art form, instilling in us the recognition that our private affairs were being placed on display. Intimate wear was pinned demurely between rows of towels and sheets to keep the prying eyes of neighbors at bay.

77

Clothes were hung by category; dishtowels pinned together like a string of cutout dolls. Bedding was hung by bed; top sheet, bottom sheet, and pillow cases lined up in a row so that, when taken down, the laundry was easy to sort by owners. Levis were placed in pant stretchers and looked as though they had rigor mortis as they danced, stiff as cowboys, in the wind. The shirts were hung upside down and when a breeze filled their bellies, they waved their arms and fought to right themselves.

My best friend and I moved into an apartment building that offered the luxury of clotheslines. I think we were nineteen years old, both dating but not yet risking more than a couple of open buttons and so we were much more concerned with dresses than underwear. I still burn with embarrassment remembering my mother's first visit to our apartment. I walked her in from the parking lot and we had to pass the clotheslines on which our laundry hung. Mother stopped, inhaled deeply on her cigarette, then vented the smoke and said, "Well, it's clear you girls are behaving yourselves. No one would show that underwear to anyone! For god's sake, get those things off the line and hang them in the shower."

When I got married, I felt drawn toward domesticity and wanted, in addition to my own washing machine, clotheslines. After a few months in an apartment in Hollywood, we moved into a charming Spanish style tri-plex in the Fairfax district that offered a fine set of clotheslines in the shared back yard. Once again, the sheets were crisp and cool, the towels scratchy and Mondays the house smelled of White King soap and fresh air, an odor that somehow allowed me to feel three-dimensional again. My clothesline expertise covered my embarrassing lack of other household skills while I mastered the art of cooking something other than spaghetti and developed an eye for dust.

When I had babies, laundry day was every day. Diapers and baby clothes were washed daily, and reverently hung. I approached early motherhood with a book by Dr. Spock and the advice of my father, an M.D., on avoiding diaper rash (no Vaseline, no Desitin, no rubber pants – just clean bottoms and air). Neither of my children ever had a rash. The price —a pile of laundry every day.

During this era of intensive laundry, I often hosted my mother-in-law from New York who adored hanging clothes. Rose was proud of her laundry experience (she leaned out her fifth story kitchen window in New York City with a mouth full of clothes pins and hung her clothes on a line strung between two apartment buildings and advanced by pulley). Rose loved hanging laundry and I always kept a line slung low for her so that, at about five feet tall, she could reach it. She hung and folded laundry willy-nilly which taught me tolerance as I felt it would be disrespectful to give her the skinny on hanging diapers.

My diapers were hung straight enough to appear ironed when taken down and folding them provided my first foray into meditation. As Rose visited for six weeks at a time, my frustration over the rumpled and poorly folded product of her help grew and I tip-toed into the baby's room late at night to re-fold diapers. Today, my clotheslines always include a low-slung line hung in memory of Rose who loved her *shiksa* daughter-in-law even after I divorced her son.

One would think that a single mother raising two children would just give in and use the dryer, but I never did. When I worked, I washed on Sunday night and hung the clothes on Monday morning so they would be dry and ready to fold when I came home from work. Clinging to my laundry tradition helped with the guilt I felt as initiator of the divorce that robbed my children of an everyday relationship with their father. In the first few months after the divorce, I took solace in doing something domestic even if it was only the laundry.

It wasn't long before I indoctrinated Ron, my second husband, into my laundry rituals. He installed clotheslines at each of our homes, even adding pull-out lines in the garage to allow for air-drying on rainy days.

I once thought my laundry fetish might be seen as an ancient art. The last time I went to the hardware store and asked for clotheslines, the young employee trying to help me looked confused. After a lengthy discussion of what a clothesline is, she lit up and exclaimed, "Oh, you want a solar dryer!" I had never heard the term.

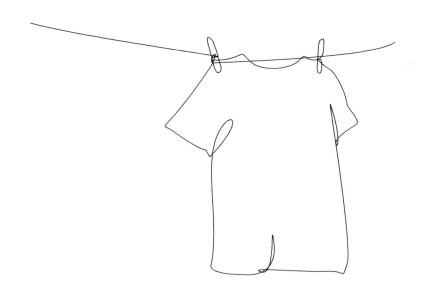

Black Lives Matter:
A Reflection About Policing
By: Steve Burns

In the last several years I have had many occasions to think about policing and how my experience of it differs so greatly from many of our black and brown neighbors and friends.

After watching so many videos of tragic intersections of police with non-white people, I reflect back on my own encounters. Strangely, Prius cars had a fairly regular problem of failing lights and there have been multiple times we had a tail light that had stopped working. The number of times that I was stopped for a tail light being out—zero. And even though I am sometimes quite late getting my new registration sticker on the license plate, I've never been stopped for that either.

Most of the interactions I have had with police have involved being pulled over—almost always for excessive speed (and the number hasn't been that large). But in all the times I was pulled over, I never had a gun pulled on me, was asked to step out of my car, or treated badly or even disrespectfully. The only time I was highly nervous was when stopped in the middle of Minnesota, and that was because the officer was afraid. Though it was a major highway, we were far from any cities, or any backup for him. I am usually flustered and nervous if pulled over, but never have the thought this could be my last day alive.

And once I had the police show up at my apartment door, quite unexpectedly. It was a typical hot Davis summer and our windows had been opened. My son was fairly young at the time and decided that we were going to eat at McDonald's that night. I informed him that we were not, and he proceeded to scream with a considerable intensity. Because I thought it might disturb the neighbors, I then closed the bedroom window and saw a woman looking up with concern from the parking lot. But when Davis's finest showed up at my door, I let them in and they gently interrogated both my children. I believe my daughter backed up my version of events and they saw no injuries on my son, so they thanked me for my patience and went on their way. I was embarrassed but never fearful that my life may be in danger.

I contrast these experiences with those of many people of color. Those who are stopped for tail lights being out, driving 'erratically' or other vague causes. Maybe selling loose cigarettes on the street or being suspicious in the toy department of a large store. Possibly even playing in the park with a toy gun. And losing their lives due to extremely aggressive and escalatory police actions—essentially shoot first and ask questions later.

Though it is difficult to face the reality of what has been happening for a long time, and realize that it is still happening in so many places and to so many people, it is now a time of reckoning that feels more serious. Our Unitarian Universalist Association has been actively working on the issue of white supremacy now for a number of years, and that has not been easy for a predominately white denomination to grapple with. It has not always been easy for me to grapple with, and to have this label that I used to only associate with those in the KKK or neo-Nazis be applied to my chosen faith. Like many, I believe my eyes are being more fully opened to how pervasive the problem is and how resistant so many of us are to these fundamental changes. May we have the courage to look around and inside ourselves.

On two ends of a spectrum are spirituality without religiosity and the other end is religiosity without spirituality. Being a Worship Associate gave me the tools and insight to navigate between the two, planning a service with enough ritual to ground the congregation but enough looseness for the magic to happen.

Stacie Hartung Frerichs

The Line Between
By: Lorraine Nail Visher

My husband and I are fond of watching sunsets. Our favorite spot is within
half a mile of our house, on Road 98, near a large Eucalyptus tree. Parked
on a gravel apron, we gaze over straight rows plowed into fallow soil or
sometimes soil ripe with tomatoes or grain. Rain puddles shimmer with oil
and grease from an old gas well that emerges from the ground behind us,
and redwing blackbirds frequent the newly planted walnut orchard to one
side. We take a bottle of wine and toast the sun as it slips behind clouds or
sinks behind the deceptively distant costal mountain range. Gazing into
those skies of fire and cream, I sometimes feel like weeping. This odd spot, a
point of tension between the natural world and the human hand, seems to be
a fitting place to stop and talk at the end of a long day.

We dream about traveling to interesting places, discuss our work, feel
ourselves growing older. Sometimes the colors before us are astounding, but
we can't avoid mentioning the level of dust in the air from overuse of the
land or wondering for the millionth time what this scene before us might
have looked like before it was cleared, drained and leveled for agriculture.
Sometimes we dip into our fears. Where is the rain we need so badly? How
bad will this global warming get? Are we doing enough, intensely enough, to
make a difference? Is it even possible?

The line between conscious urgency and outrage fatigue is thin. David and I
live in that narrow space daily. David devotes his work to agriculture and I to
education. Both are broad fields suffering from the economic depression and
the environmental degradation of these times. We are continually forced to
choose between despair and hope for the future, so we keep it small.

Working with one farmer on ways to farm more sustainably probably won't change the bigger picture, but it will create a community of hope between David and that farmer, empowering both to keep on trying. Teaching six-year-olds to treat others, including the earth, the way you want to be treated, may sound trite but it builds a classroom of respect that follows them out the schoolroom door and fuels the attitude of tomorrow's generation.

And here is what I love about sunsets: the best part comes after the sun is down. That's when all the colors bleed slowly into the horizon or explode across the clouds. That's the moment when I remember, this is what I have right now. I cannot change yesterday or control tomorrow. Every good thing we do must be done with a conscious attitude toward *sustainable* effort.

It doesn't feel like enough, but it is the only place I have to begin from. So when it's finally, fully dark, David and I still sit quietly, holding hands, while the stars come out.

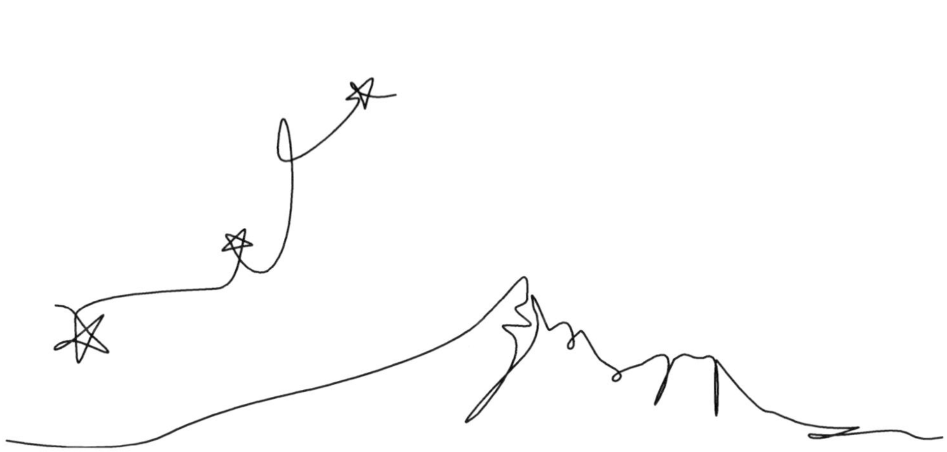

Awe
By: Sarah Larkin

Opening myself up and accepting what is given to me in the moment leaves me feeling tender, vulnerable and not in control – broken open with all of my guts on display. It doesn't sound that great, but I want to do it anyway. I can do hard things.

I love travel for this reason. Travel provides me the opportunity to exist outside of my familiar comforts. I hope to pass my thirst for adventure and travel on to my son. One of our adventures last year led us to Lassen National Park. There were hiking trails, hot springs, horses, meals, accommodations and no cell service. I love it when there is no cell service. It gives me the opportunity to operate in the world through a different type of connection. I have to rely on myself instead of a phone.

At one point during our weekend getaway, Spencer and I broke off from the hiking group. We came across a stream where folks before us had constructed paddle wheels from things they'd found nearby. They were in bits and pieces along the stream, so we went to work collecting them to see if we could get one up and running.

After a bit, I realized Spencer didn't need my help. I had A LOT of thoughts about not controlling the situation and just letting him be him in this moment.

Without my cellphone to turn to and letting go of controlling the paddle wheel build, I was left with just me. I engage in distractions every day to avoid just being, so I didn't really know how to do it.

I opened my eyes, my head and my body to my surroundings while simultaneously fighting the instinct to shut it out. I could feel the internal me struggle against the beauty of the external world.

Inhaling oxygen from the trees, feeling the warmth of the sun on my face, the coolness of the morning dew still glistening on the meadow, the peaceful sound of the babbling brook, the sight of my son exercising patience, tenacity and experiencing a connection in nature...the vibrations in my body were intense and strangely uncomfortable. I literally was having my dreams come true, and I had to deep breathe in order to continue to let it in.

This seems to be my process. I put myself in uncomfortable situations, hang out there for a while, and if I can hang on long enough, the magic comes. It's only when I break away from my self-involvement that I can truly hear what the world has to tell me. I travel to give myself the gift of perspective, dedicated time to practice receiving what the world has to say to me. The world has great wisdom to offer us, and for me to hear it, I have to be willing to strip myself down to that uncomfortable place of tender vulnerability.

Good Friday to Easter:
The Path Through Grief to Rebirth
By: Bryan Plude

On Good Friday, March 21, 2007, the day Christians recognized that Jesus was crucified, I recognized the 16th anniversary of my marriage to Becky. This Good Friday and today, Easter (and my birthday), are the most recent steps along my journey through grief to rebirth.

Easter means many different things to Unitarian Universalists. In earth-centered faiths, Easter is about rebirth after the death of winter. The historic roots of both Unitarianism and Universalism lie in Christianity, and for Christians, Easter is about the resurrection of Christ. In a metaphorical sense, are spring and resurrection so different? What I wish to talk about is my own path between these two metaphorical events—Good Friday and Easter.

My own path, and the path of my family, began with an autumn that came too soon for my wife of 15 years, Rebecca. Not yet 50, she died last October. She was taken early. Winter had begun.

Dark days followed: a funeral, two memorial services, sickness. The days grew shorter, the fog settled in, and the prolific California landscape appeared dead. Thanksgiving was difficult.

December brought two birthdays and Christmas: non-stop preparation, going through the motions for the children. On Christmas day we walked the ocean beach for the first time without Becky. The ocean was her healing place, a place we traditionally have gone during the winter since coming to California. Outside the sun shone.

January opened with storms and power outages. The house grew even colder and darker. More sickness followed. Wounded myself, I tended to needier children. What sleep there was remained troubled and restless. Three months had passed since Becky's death. I spent late nights reading, journaling, feeling my grief.

February saw more sickness and two big firsts—Valentine's Day and Rebecca's 50th birthday. With March, my neighbor, a fellow traveler, passed her first-year anniversary since her husband's death at age 47.

But in California, spring has broken. During the darkest days of winter native grasses sprout with life-giving rain. So, too, on my journey. Becky's memorial services were beautiful and life-affirming for the many who mourned her. Support from church members, neighbors and friends has made the difficult job of single parenting easier, warming my heart, knowing we are loved. My sister's family provided light on Thanksgiving by hosting us. The girls' art bereavement classes were enormously helpful. My own support group shared more laughter and fewer tears. Becky's 50th birthday was filled with the support and laughter of good friends.

I do not remember if I sustained hope during the dark days immediately following Becky's death. I do know that it was not too long before the spark was born. That spark has been sustained and grown with the help and love of many people. Unlike Jesus' resurrection, my own rebirth is taking more than three days. It is not complete today. It may very well not be complete by next Easter, or the following one. But it is happening.

Ponder
By: Susan Steinbach

I invite you now into a time of stillness. Now is the time for putting aside the burdens that you carry. Relax your body, close your eyes if you'd like to. Let a deep breath fill your lungs. Find inside that still quietness that escapes us in real time.

Ponder the late season hummingbird

that came to the window this morning

looking for the red berries and nectar that has vanished.

Ponder the look she gave us.

Where is her partner? Her nest?

Will she survive the bracing winter?

Have the sense to take shelter?

Ponder the harvest moon that appeared

flooding the treetops with light,

rendering night into day

tracing an ancient, timeless path

across the heavens. Oh, golden orb,

We notice and comply. Rapture is so simple

in your presence.

Ponder the still black crow that lies down

on the wet grass by the vineyard

and looks helplessly our way.

He knows he will not survive the day.

Our footsteps do not frighten him.

We feel compassion. He lies obedient to gravity, accepting.

Soon, his body will rejoin the earth.

Ponder the golden rain trees along the roadway

bursting gold and amber at the end of autumn.

Prepare our hearts for trunks with clean branches.

Silhouettes without leaves.

Puddles of fresh rain.

Fog on olive trees.

Birds that stay north.

Ponder the hummingbird, the moon, the crow, the golden rain trees.

Such beauty is laid at our feet daily. Gifts for the taking.

My Secret Friend Barbara
By: Emily Burstein

I have been reading much more since (the catastrophic election of) November 2016. For courage and insight. And to feel the words in my bones. I usually listen to audiobooks. My experience is more embodied when I listen. I enjoy mostly fiction with strongly drawn characters, some whom I wish I could converse with for hours. The non-fiction I enjoy most is memoirs. I absorb information better through peoples' lived experiences. Most often I listen while walking the dog. It is like a walking meditation but with more distractions.

I just finished listening to a book by Barbara Kingsolver. I adore her - she is like a secret friend. Her characters have the same essential yearnings, joys, and fears that I experience in my own life. When I listen to her words my breath often catches unexpectedly.

Her books celebrate the natural world in all its awesomeness, and they raise up our UU mantra of the inherent worth and dignity of every person. Her words connect me to my own strength. They bring me self-compassion and compassion for others. They call me to be responsible for our earth.

My secret friend Barbara Kingsolver was with me recently when I phone banked for Joe Biden. An older man from Virginia felt rage so strong that I felt heat in my ear. He told me he used to be a lifelong Democrat. Now he is voting for Trump, because, "they" are tearing down the monuments. I thought of the foul-mouthed grandpa in one of Kingsolver's books. His disappointments shrank his once hopeful heart to a bitter shell. I took a slow breath and continued my calls.

Kingsolver brought me help again when I couldn't navigate a difficult conversation with my son without putting him on the defensive. I felt a thorny mixture of weariness and anger. Then, I thought of the irresistible mom, named Willa, in one of Kingsolver's books. She held her complicated family together with love, spunk and duct tape, yet she had let her adult children down a lot when they were young. I remembered Willa and collected up some humor and patience for my own challenges.

Kingsolver paints the natural world with the same complexity and wonder she brings to her characters. She threads her stories with feisty folks that fiercely love and protect our fragile planet. These friends remind me to savor the luscious fragrance of lavender in my garden and wage my own small battles for our earth.

My reading is a necessity and a practice. I crave words that are deeply felt and authentic. It brings me into connection with my own sacredness and the sacredness of others. It gives me the strength and curiosity to confront our shattered world. Reading helps me put one foot in front of another, which right now, is a lot.

103

A Sacred Covenant of Unconditional Love, Respect and Trust

By: Lily Roberts

Two Trees by Janet Miles

>*A portion of your soul has been*
>
>*entwined with mine*
>
>*A gentle kind of togetherness, while*
>
>*separately we stand.*
>
>*As two trees deeply rooted in*
>
>*separate plots of ground,*
>
>*While their topmost branches*
>
>*come together,*
>
>*Forming a miracle of lace*
>
>*against the heavens.*

A while back I was working on a very sacred Covenant with my husband, Robert Bakke. We decided some time ago that on our 35th wedding anniversary, we would have a recommitment ceremony. We had considered the little chapel at Sea Ranch where we had vacationed many times since March 1983. However, we decided to renew our marital covenant here in the Unitarian Universalist Church of Davis, our new spiritual home. In March 1983, we concluded our personal wedding vows with "This marriage represents our continuing commitment to an open, honest, changing, and progressive relationship." Our covenant was, and still is, one of love, family, friendship, and support for one another.

In September 2016, Reverend Morgan McLean wrote: "In my experience, a covenant is an opportunity to enter a sacred relationship, based on a deep sense of respect and trust." Morgan, of course, was talking about our church community, but those words were clearly relevant to the covenant of marriage and commitment to another person.

As I continue my own spiritual journey, I often reflect on our monthly themes. So, what does covenant mean to me? How does the theme of intention relate to renewing my marital covenant? Like the trees in the poem, Robert and I have stood separately and independently, and yet, we now stand with our branches intertwined. The lace of our past 35 years represents how we have lived with intention to fulfill our covenant.

The tapestry of our lives was formed by risks taken and experiences lived. In 1981, Robert fell in love with me, a young widow, who had a 3-year old bi-racial daughter. He wooed her as much as he did me. His love was true for both of us. After we married, he adopted her, and continued to raise her as his own. In 1986, we were blessed with a baby boy.

In 1993, Robert collapsed at our gym. He was on the treadmill next to our daughter and he fell backward. His heart stopped; he had flat lined. I was already in the locker room and our young son was in the daycare. Miraculously, he was brought back to life by the quick-thinking EMT on staff, and then rushed off in an ambulance.

Lying in bed that first night with our children on either side of me, I was frightened. I had already been widowed once at a young age. But I knew that our family would make it through this horrifying event. A few days later, Robert had a quintuple bypass to repair arteries clogged by genetic imperfections. His recovery took months, but through it all our family's love and support, no matter what, prevailed.

We have experienced transformations, joys, and sorrows. Like the story told by the rings of trees, we have grown together, and apart, and back together many times. Our covenant has helped us weather many tough situations, but more importantly, we learned to appreciate and savor the little things – the tiny miracles, like dew on a leaf that reveals a miniature rainbow when struck, just so, by the sun.

Living our covenant, we have reaped great rewards; our two children are now successful, happily married, and not living at home! And we have a zest for life that has not waned in retirement. We have evolved as individuals, as a couple, as friends, lovers, and parents. The complexities of who we are and how we transform over time must be respected.

Our new covenant needed to embrace these changes as we become ever more deeply intertwined. Perhaps, leaning into each other more, our trunks will become less stable, our minds less agile, but our hearts will be forever committed. It is our intention that we focus on the coming years as a period of balance, reflection, and peace. Our renewed covenant will be an extension of our spiritual journey together. As always, we will focus on family, and love and support one another, no matter what.

As Unitarian Universalists, we intend to continue our journey *"living within a spiritual community with actions based on respectful conversation, receptive listening, and open-hearted presence.*[7]*"*

Stillness
By: Cliff Ohmart

Growing up on a small farm in Upstate New York in the 1950s and 60s helped me appreciate why someone would come up with the description 'The Bleak Mid-Winter'. Back then, the snow was on the ground from November to April and during the short days of late December and January, one could get a feeling of bleakness, at least for adults. From my perspective, I loved growing up with snowy winters. There was a sense of adventure and magic.

Some of my most memorable moments were when night-time temperatures approached 20 degrees below zero. I would go outside in the morning into the blinding sunshine and snowy white wonderland. It was so cold my nose and lungs would sting when I breathed. The snow underfoot would squeak loudly with every step. Even though it was a clear blue, cloudless sky, the little bit of moisture that was in the air would crystalize and float gently to the ground sparkling in the sunshine as it went. It was like being in a real-life snow globe. When I stood still, I would be overcome with an incredible sense of stillness.

Snow has the ability to create stillness for me.

Another memorable winter experience, this time when I had moved to California, was when I drove from Berkeley to the Sierras one afternoon in April to do some field work at Blodgett Experimental Forest. When I got there, the ground was bare. I went to bed in the bunkhouse and slept very soundly. In the morning, as I woke up, I gradually became aware of an incredible sense of silence. I went outside and saw that about six inches of snow was covering everything. It was as if I had woken up in a completely different world. The stillness covered me like a blanket. It was magical. I was overcome with a wonderful feeling of peace.

Over the years I appreciate stillness more and more. It refreshes me and restores my hope for things. My favorite place to find it now is at a campground near Eagle Lake in Northern California. I have many fond memories of camping and fishing there with my son Joel as he grew into an adult. I continue to go by myself and discovered that if I go after Labor Day, the weather is still magnificent and often I am one of only two or three others in the entire campground. I spend much of my time sitting in my camp chair under the majestic Ponderosa pines that soar above me and let the stillness envelope me. When the sun begins to go down everything turns golden. It's magic.

Amazingly, during those periods of stillness, my mind does not race around thinking of all sorts of things nor does it try to solve my or the world's problems. It simply relaxes and takes in the stillness. For me stillness does wonders. I highly recommend it!

It was the experience of working with the ministers, Beth and Morgan, and the other Worship Associates that brought me the greatest satisfaction. Of course, writing the reflections, and then presenting them, took me into myself, and forced me to write down all the thoughts that were wheeling around in my mind. As a Worship Associate, I felt much more of a contributing part of the congregation, and I was glad for that.

Elli Norris

Grief, Hope and Love
By: Lee Ann D'Amato Raymond

In her groundbreaking book, "On Death and Dying", psychiatrist Elizabeth Kubler Ross discusses her theory of the five stages of grief. She once said about the death of a loved one that "The reality is that you will grieve forever. You will not 'get over' the loss of a loved one; you will learn to live with it. You will heal and you will rebuild yourself around the loss you have suffered. You will be whole again but you will never be the same. Nor should you be the same nor would you want to."

When my sister Nina died of AIDS-related pneumonia at the age of 30, it was a loss unlike any I had ever known. When she died in 1989, not very much was known about AIDS. In fact, when Nina went into San Francisco General Hospital, the doctors had just recently stopped wearing full body protection and masks when entering the room of an AIDS patient. The only drug was AZT, which was ineffective in Nina's case because it was prescribed too late.

She had been sick a long time but did not know what her illness was. She went into the hospital three days before she died, and I didn't even know she was dying. I wasn't ready. I couldn't deal with it. I wasn't even able to say goodbye because the idea of losing my only sister, my best friend, was too much.

I was at her bedside that last night she was able to speak to us. She spent the whole night telling me her hopes and dreams for me and my sons. She wanted me to start acting again. I had stopped because my sons were two and five. She wanted me to live a good, full, and happy life.

113

When Nina died, I was gutted. At the beginning, I could not think about anything but my grief. But eventually I began thinking about what she had said to me that night when it was just the two of us in her hospital room. Eventually I realized that my best gift to her would be to live a full and happy life because hers was cut short, so I went to counseling and I reached out to friends.

It was my best friend Larry Torres who really helped me through my sister's death. He would come over every day and make sure I ate and got dressed. He loved my kids. He would bring over groceries and take them out every Saturday to go to a movie and to Toys r Us. Larry was just a really lovely person, full of joy and life. And he made me laugh. I would not have made it through my grief if it had not been for Larry.

Sadly, about six months after Nina died, Larry too started getting sick. He had extremely high blood pressure and was hospitalized numerous times over the following five years. Larry had a stroke at the young age of 28, and after brain surgery, died on the same date as my sister, just five years later.

I was devastated but when Larry was in the hospital for the final time, his surgeon came to me to tell me that Larry was not going to make it, that he knew it would not be a successful surgery. He said that he chose to tell me because he could tell "I could handle it". It was a gift the surgeon gave me. He could see that I would survive this loss too.

What I have learned about grief is that if you have even one person in your life who loves you and sees you through the painful stages of loss, you will be okay. I learned there is wisdom to be gained on the other side of grief -

that the hope and love Larry showed me had sustained me through the five years since Nina was gone and would sustain me through both his loss and the rest of my life.

Because of Nina and Larry's love, I am changed. I am not the same person, but I am whole.

A Lily Among Roses
By: Lily Roberts

With a name like Lily, the Unitarian Universalist Flower Communion[8] feels like a celebration of who I am – a unique member of a diverse yet welcoming community of flowers. My first name is actually Lily Lee. I was named after my grandmother, Lillian, and my godmother, Lela. By third grade, I dropped the Lee when writing my name at school and became just plain Lily.

When I was young, Lily was not a common little girl's name like it is now. I was teased about my name; kids would call me Willy Wee instead of Lily Lee. Other kids would say hurtful things, like "Where's your frog, Lily pad?" These words made me feel like I did not belong and made me sad. No one wants to feel alone.

To me, heaven is a field of lilies and other flowers touched softly by a light breeze and buzzing with the sound of honey bees on a sunny day. I recall fondly when I was five years old, lying on my back in the grass with my best friend, Angela Hernandez. We were looking up at an unusually blue sky in Fort Lewis, Washington. I remember sharing that I felt like we were inside a big blue bubble. Angela taught me how to say words in Spanish, like *azul* for blue or *amiga* for friend. And she told me that her name meant Angel. Angela and I would watch the honey bees on the clover. And then, we would walk carefully so as not to step on them.

We chased away other kids who tried to capture bees in glass jars. And then, we would find a bee-free spot and sit down, and *mi amiga* would teach me more words in Spanish. I don't know what happened to Angela because I moved away, but I think of her every now and then – recalling our blue

117

bubble friendship. My desire to study Spanish and Italian began with that young friendship, when an angel and a flower were lying in the grass and imagining life inside a big blue bubble – no harmful words, no biases, just friends – we felt safe together.

Fast forward to 18 years old, and my best friend's name was Lupita. She was of Mexican heritage, like Angela. And like me, she was first generation in her family to go to college. That summer, I met a diversity of students of color who were beginning their university studies too. We were in an Educational Opportunity Program – I was there because of my low-income status while many others were there as minority, first-time college students. I was a lily among roses, orchids, irises, and daisies. We had the occasional chrysanthemum try to stir up trouble, but our beautiful bouquet was a community bound together by our desire to obtain a college degree and improve our lives – and we felt safe together.

Fast forward to today, and I have many friends who, like a field of wild flowers, vary in age, gender, race and ethnicity. They live from California to Washington in the north, across the country to states along the east coast, and even more live across the Atlantic Ocean in Italy and Sweden! Here in this Sanctuary, I am one flower among many today. I am not alone and I feel safe!

Joy and Woe are Woven Fine
By: Steve Burns

Family is sacred to me because it is the incubator where we are formed, and what we adults form to bring new life into this world. It is my refuge and research laboratory where, when my children were little, I kept trying different experiments to get the results I wanted. Those with toddlers or teenagers may understand this science.

Who I am was created in my family, which is an ever-dynamic organism. This is not to say that family is always easy, as joy and woe are frequently woven fine.

When I had just begun a very intense engineering school, the first weekend after classes I drove 12 hours for a close friend's wedding. Thus, I was behind in my homework from the start and it took months to catch up. I was incredibly stressed, but being a guy, I couldn't easily admit that to anyone. So despite the precious time taken from studying, by the time Thanksgiving arrived, I knew that home was the only place to be. Exhausted and brittle from the strain, I finally relaxed and slept soundly in my parent's home. Just being with them made an immense difference in my resilience for the remainder of the academic term.

My older brother Chuck was a self-proclaimed bachelor, so of course he married early. He had many male buddies, so he chose Dad as his best man. I did the same, though my reason was slightly different, being that most of my closest friends were women. Multiple sons choosing their father as their best man is an unusual tradition, but one that my younger brother continued. My Dad taught us to be men—balancing a demanding career while still helping raise five children and caring for an ailing wife. He was the best man at every one of his son's weddings.

One of my most wondrous days was the birth of my first child, Laura. I still vividly remember the elevator ride in the hospital shortly after her delivery when I was overflowing with joy. The faces of others in the elevator displayed concern, worry and sadness. Their visits to the hospital were for very different reasons than the birth of a beautiful child. Joy and woe <u>are</u> woven together. That day was also my grandfather's last, and even going back to Nebraska to join with the extended family to grieve his death and honor his life, I was still filled with joy of our newborn's life. I could barely contain my excitement as I met with my cousins, showing them pictures of our lovely Laura. It was a powerful mix of emotions, and a time that stands still in my memories.

My experience of family continues with a new generation. In the last few years, we have been visiting as often as possible with my son and his family, which includes our two grandsons Mendel and Sruli. I love holding them, looking into their eyes, and sharing in their discovery of the world. Studying their features, I detect traces of their ancestors; whose eyes, ears, lips, and hair do they have? Watching their temperament and reactions, I can both observe and attempt to gently shape their development. It is an immense joy being a grandparent, as many already know. If you still have grandparents, you may not realize how important you are to them or how much they might be able to teach you.

I hope and work for a world that will be worthy for my children, grandchildren, and yours.

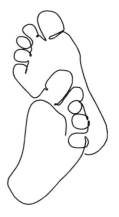

The Importance of Collective Action
By: Marty West

I am a strong supporter of collective action by workers and have been involved in the labor movement throughout my professional life. But I have never actually worked in a unionized job. At the research university, where I worked, faculty do not regard themselves as "workers" and see no need for unions. Despite this widespread attitude, I have found that collective action is necessary and can be successful in other contexts.

The context where I have been successful in organizing collective action has been in seeking equality for women faculty. The interesting twist, however, is that the focus of our collective action has not been the university administration, but has been our faculty colleagues. Let me explain.

As a University of California faculty member, my employment terms were set by the faculty members in my department, not by the campus administration. I was hired by a vote of the law faculty. They set my rank at hire, which determined my starting salary. The tenured faculty later voted to grant me tenure, which came with a higher rank and salary. Even after faculty achieve tenure, the department's faculty continue to vote on each other's promotions and salary raises.

In 1994, responding to pressure from women faculty, the UCD administration conducted a salary review to determine whether women faculty received salaries equal to men's. Nationwide, women faculty were paid about 10% less than men. The campus study found similar differences at UC Davis.

After these preliminary findings, the UCD administration turned the salary equity issue over to the faculty's campus Committee on Academic Personnel (CAP). As CAP began to design procedures to conduct individual equity reviews of women faculty's files, a group of conservative faculty attacked the study, claiming that women received lower salaries because they were less productive, publishing less research. "Women faculty simply deserved less pay," they said.

The opponents of the equity reviews claimed the reviews by CAP would undermine the faculty "peer review" process. So the conservative faculty obtained the signatures of 62 professors (59 men and 3 women) on a petition demanding a vote by the entire faculty, a vote by mail, to stop CAP from doing the reviews. All current faculty, and all retired faculty, were allowed to vote. At that time, women were 20% of the current faculty, but only 10% of the retired faculty. The conservatives won this first round: 527 faculty voted to stop the equity reviews, 503 faculty voted to allow them to go forward.

That's when we worked to organize the women faculty. The battle moved to the faculty's Academic Senate representative assembly. A special meeting was called. By this time we had over 50 faculty women on our e-mail list, and we assigned women to talk to the faculty representatives from each department.

At the special meeting, women faculty packed the meeting to talk about the difficulties they faced. Although most of us women faculty could not vote, we could tell our stories. It was an emotional meeting lasting over two hours. Then someone called for a show of a quorum. The quorum had evaporated by that time, so the meeting adjourned without a vote.

126

We had to organize all over again! The second special meeting was rescheduled for Valentines Day. We now had 70 women on our e-mail list, and this time the majority of the people in the room were faculty women. Our prearranged parliamentary strategy worked, a vote was taken, and we won: 31 faculty representatives voted "yes" to allow CAP to proceed with the equity reviews, and 18 representatives voted "no."

It took another year for CAP to actually conduct the equity reviews of the files of those women faculty who requested such a review. By the fall of 1996, 38 women faculty at UC Davis had received a salary increase. More importantly, the campus adopted a new system to review all faculty salaries at hire. Now, new women assistant professors at UCD make 96% of what entry-level faculty men make, compared to only 92% at other UC campuses.

I believe that through collective action we really can make a difference. Through collective action, the power of one is multiplied four-fold! [9]

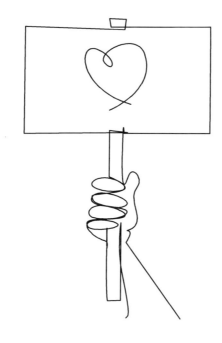

Knowing the Right Road
By: Elli Norris

I'm relieved that the topic for today was titled "Infinite Roads Diverge," departing from Robert Frost's "Two roads diverged…." As I thought back over roads I've traveled in my life, the image that came to mind was of many-colored balls of yarn that a family of kittens had been playing with. Picture it!

Then I began to think about how I had ended up on some roads and not others. Had I made a choice? Frost never uses the word "choice." He says, "took" the one, and not the other. You know, I think that feels more true to me—I "took" this road, not that one. I mean, did I stand there deliberating and then "take" one of the roads?

Sure, often I did. But other times I seem to have **known** which one I was going to take, even before I ever thought about it all that much. It was more like a given. Some might say, it was like hearing a "call."

Here's an example of one of those.

In my early 40s I was living in Los Gatos with a small practice in psychotherapy and massage. I had just returned from a three-month holistic healing program at Esalen Institute at Big Sur and—I was lonesome! I missed being in such a healing community. Could I find such a thing again?

The answer came from a friend who asked me: "Have you ever heard of the Desert?

No, I never had, but I knew instantly that's where I wanted to be. She explained that the Desert was a non-denominational retreat house in Berkeley supported by a liberal United Methodist Church. Its founders called it the Desert to make a point—you don't have go to the silence of the desert to retreat to the silence of the Desert.

Within weeks I was living in the Desert in Berkeley, working with others to offer peaceful retreat time to other seekers in the middle of the city.

Did I deliberate over taking this road? No. I knew, and there I was, on this new road. Unfortunately, while we all had very good intentions and good hearts, we had no financial sense at all and the Desert closed after only two or three years. But taking this road was a life-changing experience for me.

Ten years later another "call" arrived. Go home to the family ranch in the foothills of the Southern Sierra which I inherited after my mother died. That's another choice I "knew" was the right one. And 19 years later, I "knew' it was time to move on, and here I am in Davis and at UU Church of Davis.

Now, in my elder years, roads still diverge before me. So many troubles in the world and right here at home… which shall I give energy to? Do I have energy to give much at all? If not, what shall I do?

I'm afraid age does NOT bring all the answers with it. But I'll rely on my life experience. Answers do come. Sometimes they come after due consideration. And sometimes I just seem to KNOW which road to take.

I'm waiting.

My Worship Associate experiences were certainly an important part of my evolving consciousness. Being a Worship Associate provided me a rich opportunity to be generative rather than a passive part of the congregation.

Kirk Ridgeway

The Wisdom of Crows
By: Susan Steinbach

I reside on campus in the thick walnut trees at the Experimental Farm, at least in the daytime. At night, I seek refuge at University Mall, not Starbuck's, but the tops of trees along Russell Boulevard, with countless black-feathered friends. I've been told we make a lot of noise when we gather at dusk and that the cars that pass under us get upset at our 'droppings'. Geesh, what's a crow to do?

I noticed her last week, that skinny redheaded human who's been coming to Experimental Farm for years. She usually parks her bike away from the walnut trees, and when she drives, she always avoids parking near my haunt. She never looks up at me. She came really early last week, just after dawn, something about a busload of Japanese students leaving the Farm forever. I guess the humans call the Farm 'Extension Center'. Anyway, she was waving goodbye to them, then came down her usual road by the walnut trees to unlock the office. She stopped, she looked, and in the distance, she spotted something she never saw before – the flock of wild turkeys that frequent our domain.

I've never seen her pause like that. Her jaw was hanging open. The turkeys are here almost every morning, competing with my crow friends for the food scraps on the compost piles at the Farm. *"How do you like them apples?"* I blurted out. She was looking at those turkeys like she's never looked at me. *"What beautiful birds!"* she uttered. *"I had no idea you lived here – under my nose! How could I have missed you!"* she gasped. The turkeys kept pecking at the compost piles in the morning mist, but she stood motionless, watching those big birds, as if she couldn't get enough of them. I was jealous.

133

I dropped a walnut near her feet, hoping she'd look up at me the same way she was looking at those turkeys. *"I'm beautiful too!"* I cawed out. But in an instant, the human was gone again, into her office, never to notice the common crows like me who populate her world..[10]

Growing up Catholic
By: Stacie Hartung-Frerichs

It was a hot summer day, not unlike today, when I was escaping the heat in the pool of a friend's home, a fellow UU, about 15 years ago. I don't think I knew what Unitarian Universalism was or even that she was part of the congregation. As we were swimming and talking about our beliefs and religion, my friend said, "I never understood the Catholic part about a virgin birth, it's a nice myth but a virgin birth?"

Wow, in the cool water of the pool, in the heat of the summer, she just rocked my world. I was raised Catholic. Not that I hadn't questioned many church teachings, including not allowing women priests, the strict social doctrine on reproductive rights and exclusiveness of those "welcomed into heaven", but I never thought to question a virgin birth!

Maybe I never thought deeply about it, or maybe I singled out and focused on the parts of Catholicism I liked: treating your neighbor as you would like to be treated, Jesus welcoming everyone and altogether just not judging others.

Just a few days ago, I read a headline in an article about Pope Francis, "Pope Francis has had doubts about the Christian faith".

In the article, Pope Francis states when talking about suffering and evil, "Many times I find myself in a crisis of faith….Sometimes I've questioned Jesus: 'But why do you allow this?' " The Pope has had these thoughts of doubt as "a boy, a seminarian, a priest, a bishop and even now as Pope", he admitted.

His allowing for questioning and doubt within the Catholic Church has been a break from his predecessors.

In UUism our beliefs are diverse and inclusive. We have no shared creed. Our shared covenant supports "the free and responsible search for truth and meaning."

Unitarian Universalists believe more than one thing. We think for ourselves and reflect together about important questions about:

- the existence of a higher power,
- life and death,
- the meaning of sacred texts,
- where we go for inspiration and guidance,
- and the roles of prayer and spiritual practice.

Back to that conversation in the pool, I still can't believe that I didn't question a fundamental doctrine of the Catholic Church. Since then, I also have gone on my own faith and belief journey.

I am not finished,

I am not sure I even know where I am but I have found this community, here, that respects my journey of discovery.

Starting Over
By: Sarah Larkin

Destruction is a key force in the practice of starting over and rebuilding. A fire that decimated my home, treasures, furniture, and took the lives of our animals - REQUIRED me to rebuild my life. I had to say goodbye to so much.

When we started over, my wife, our son and I were the recipients of an abundance of generosity in many forms - warm embraces, meals, clothes, cards.

My father is an architect. He spent countless hours walking us through the process, made monthly trips up from LA and redesigned our house for us in a way that far better suited our needs. The Sunday after we lost our home, we came to this church for the very first time and left with a meal train. Complete strangers took care of us. It was truly unbelievable. I experienced incredible feelings of humility, grace and a deep feeling of awe at the outpouring of support.

Our new home was rebuilt with custom everything. We splurged on seaglass tile, double ovens, stone countertops in the kitchen, an electric fireplace to warm the cozy living room. Sliding glass doors led to a deck with an outdoor lounge area, and a hot tub in the backyard. Did I mention the hot tub? We had to make every decision together to rebuild our home, but the deep pain and sorrow we experienced served as a seemingly impenetrable wedge that followed us into our new home.

When we moved back in, we were both still so lost. The time came for me to say goodbye and thank you to my relationship of 16 years, give up my newly rebuilt house, give up sharing my son's life 50% of the time, and invest in myself and my career.

The end of all that once was left a vast expanse in me. I had two choices - let it swallow me up or fill it up. I chose to learn about myself, to think about how I want to interact in the world and what steps are required of me to *BE* that way in the world.

Starting over has led to an acceptance and love for myself that the old version did not have.

The relationships I have built grow stronger and deeper as I encourage and celebrate vulnerability and acknowledge the imperfection of life. Starting over again and again and again gives me freedom from indecision and doubt because I know that I can always start over, adjust, or take a break and start again. I am empowered to know that I will never truly fail if I have the willingness to fail and the courage to always start again.

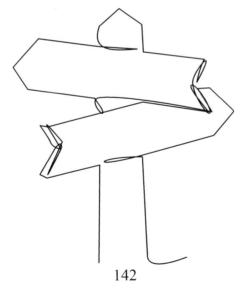

Setting Intentions
By: Cliff Ohmart

I am sitting on a bed in a cramped room in a hole-in-the-wall motel in Omak, Washington, a town of maybe a couple hundred people. Main street is the highway through town, about 20 feet from my motel room door. The room shakes slightly when trucks go by. There is a statue of an oversized rearing horse in front of the motel, which I guess is appropriate because I am staying in the Mustang Inn. I am almost 40, a successful research scientist for the Australian government, yet I am here in the USA checking out a job that pays about half what I am making down under. My wife and young son are halfway around the world in Canberra waiting to hear how I am doing. I am thinking 'How on earth did I get to this point in my life?'

Many years later, when I was working with winegrape growers, encouraging them to use sustainable farming practices in their vineyards, I had a favorite saying I would share with them to illustrate what I thought was an important point. It was a rough translation of something Yogi Berra said. For those of you that don't know who he was, he was a catcher for the New York Yankees baseball team and was infamous for his non-sequiturs. The saying goes something like this: If you don't know where you are going, you may end up someplace else.

Well, looking back on that night in Omak, Washington, I had ended up at that 'someplace else'. However, up until a few years before then, I knew very well where I wanted to go. Since my undergraduate days, I knew I wanted to end up as a professor of forest entomology. I knew where I had been, where I was and where I wanted to go. My intentions were clear. I would finish my PhD as quickly as possible, get a research job to establish a reputation and then when a professorship opened up, I would pounce on it. Spin the clock forward to that night in Omak, Washington and it was clear my best intentions had failed.

How does this story end? Well, my family and I had to reset the 'where are we going' and then establish new intentions of how to get there. It worked. I guess we did end up 'someplace else' but it matched with the new 'where we wanted to go'.

In thinking about the process that the Unitarian Universalist Church of Davis is in the midst of and relating it the major life experience I just described, I've come to the conclusion that the 'how do we get there' part maybe the most challenging of the whole process. Intentions can be scary to embark on, because they might be anxiety provoking, take longer than we think, or in the end may not get us to where we thought we were going, like what happened in my situation. Yet I kept moving forward, recalibrating when necessary, and I ended up where I wanted to be.

[Being a Worship Associate] has helped me clarify my thoughts at times, revealed more about myself to the congregation and helped me practice my writing skills.

Steve Burns

The Wisdom of Years
By: Joan Stek

When I was invited to find pearls of wisdom in my past and talk about them, my first reaction was to laugh … there are no pearls in my past! But of course, I did learn some things over all those years and I'm happy to share a few of those. So here goes.

I was born a long time ago, in 1927 in the Netherlands which made my teenage years right in the middle of World War II, during the five years of Nazi Germany's occupation in our country. That was the most eventful period of my life - many memories and also many things I learned. Some examples: an abhorrence of violence in all its forms, of people against people, most of all the violence that one regime can commit against its neighboring countries. It is really crazy! When will we ever learn?

Another thing I learned: material possessions are not important. We lost all our stuff in the war but came out with our lives intact. And my goodness, life is so much more important than things.

And then I found another thing that stayed with me from that time which is not beneficial at all: an irrational and silly prejudice against anything German. That should have worn off in these 80 plus years but it didn't. That got me to thinking – probably many people have strange twists in their mind just like me. And I should be more understanding of other folks' weird ideas. (I'm thinking of course of people at the far other end of the political spectrum.)

Anyway – then there was the exciting time of liberation and recovery such as the reopening of the universities, my entry in university and earning a medical degree. This brings me to one little pearl: the practice of medicine is just about the best career anyone could aspire to. The intellectual challenge plus the knowledge of doing something worthwhile is a combination that can't be beat. I heartily recommend the medical field to any young person contemplating his or her future.

After marriage, moving to Canada, then New Jersey and Massachusetts, starting a family and re-entering medicine I finally found Unitarianism in California in a Fellowship east of Sacramento. It was a joyful discovery – a belief I could agree with, a good religious education program and a whole bunch of like-minded people. Ultimately, here at this church, I found my niche in the caring committee. Looking back this caring for other people has been a general "theme" for life that I can recommend. It may not be a pearl and may be simple and "pedestrian" but caring for one's fellow human being is a worthwhile principle to live by (after family and work). Even now in my old age, when I sometimes feel down or sorry for myself, there is a perfect cure – I go visit one of my lonely old friends and find both of our worlds are a little brighter.

Maybe now I'm in my last few years, I may need caring myself someday. If that ever happens, I hope that will be for a very short time only.

A River Called Mystery
By: Mary Higgins MacDonnell

Today we are thinking about the many ways in which this time of year is experienced as holy.

It's the Spring Equinox for the Earth-based religions. Jews are observing Passover. Christians are celebrating Easter and the resurrection. And this year, Easter coincides with the Muslim month of Ramadan.

Speaking of the various sources which we draw from in our Unitarian Universalist tradition raised the question for me, "What do I believe?" That lead me to the following quote attributed to a Sufi master,

> *"A river passes through many countries, and each claims it for its own. But there is only one river." – Sufi Wisdom*

As a Unitarian Universalist, I call this river Mystery. I call the river Seeking with Joy and Hope. This river is my desire to find meaning in my earthly existence.

I remember a conversation I had with my then healthy and ninety-something year old mother. We were pondering what happens to people after death. She had a firm faith in the afterlife and heaven; I wasn't so sure.

We made a pact that whoever should die first would come back and contact the remaining one to describe the afterlife. My mother passed away in 2015, and so far, no message.

But I have received one message from the "other side".

In the 1980's, when I was working as a labor and delivery nurse I made friends with Louise, another nurse.   Louise was a strong feminist. She and I were both applying to the graduate program to become nurse-midwives. She was smart, funny and irreverent. We became fast friends. For the next seven years we hung out, had adventures and laughed a lot. Then, we had a falling out. I wish my skills in handling conflict had been better, but it was not to be.

She eventually moved to another town, and I didn't see her anymore. Some years passed.   One day I ran into a mutual friend of ours on the street. She was anxious to share her news, "Did you hear that Louise died?" Louise had been living quite a while with a chronic form of leukemia, but died unexpectedly one day. This friend and I chatted some more then parted. This news was very striking. You see, I had experienced a sort of "encounter" about a week prior, and the timing of that did coincide with when Louise had died.

The encounter was a feeling and some words. The feeling came over me, quite peacefully, and captured my attention. I found myself thinking of Louise.   The words I recall clearly, "I forgive you. I release you".   It was not me talking to Louise. It was Louise talking to me. The words were characteristic of her way of speaking. I have no doubt that I received a visit from Louise, possibly as she was leaving this earthly existence.

Is this evidence of an afterlife?

I'm still unsure, and that's okay. Remember, my river is called Mystery.

152

[Being a Worship Associate] deepened my inquiry into domains
I may have previously never considered.

Kirk Ridgeway

My son Paul, My blessing
By: Lee Ann D'Amato Raymond

The idea of writing about blessings for me has been a difficult one. I have never felt particularly blessed in my life. There are moments in my life that certainly were wonderful, but the concept of being blessed is just hard for me to accept.

When my sons were 12 and 10, I became a single mother. It was a rough time in my life, both financially and emotionally, but this period allowed me to become very close to my sons since I had primary custody, and their father did not take them all of the times that he was scheduled to have them. I worried about my oldest child Paul the most because he has always been an emotional soul, and he seemed especially affected.

One night, about a year after his dad and I split up, Paul came to me and told me that he was gay, that he was not interested in girls. I wish I could say that I reacted like the liberal mother I considered myself to be. I mean, after all, I grew up in Berkeley in the 60's amidst a political climate of openness and change. But I knew of no one in my family who was gay. I had no experience with it. When I envisioned Paul's life as a man, it included a wife and children. I basically told him that this might change. He had never been on a date after all. Even reading my own words now, I cringe at how little I knew or understood.

He told me that he had known his feelings since he was about five. When he told his best friend, I watched my son, who loved his friend and his friend's family, be completely rejected by them. They said he wasn't safe to be around - a family he had babysat for and spent time with since kindergarten. He was devastated, and I was crushed for him.

We continued to have many conversations over the years about his homosexuality. He tells me about his dates, what it is like to be a young gay man. He has many female friends, but he has always known who he is. He is the person who has most opened me up to the world. Through Paul's eyes, I have seen a side of life that I would not have known in the same way - from Gay Pride to the Supreme Court ruling on marriage equality - we talk about it all. He reminded me the morning of the ruling that this is just one step in the fight for human rights in the LGBTQ community, that they still face discrimination in housing and employment in some states. He said that we must keep up the good fight.

Paul has made me a more loving and giving person. A more accepting soul. He is one of the least prejudiced people I have ever known. He challenges me every day to fight for the rights of others. My son, my Paul, my blessing.

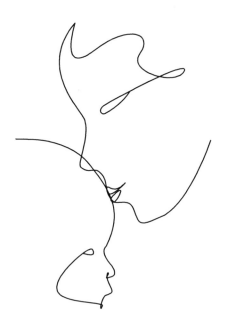

Planting History: Ruminations on Rumi
By: Karen Klussendorf Kurth

"Don't think the garden loses its ecstasy in the winter. It's quiet but the roots are down there riotous." -Rumi

The life of soil – an entire ecosystem that is 50% solid and 50% pore space. Organic matter, silt, sand, minerals, air, water, living organisms and clay, all of which interact slowly yet constantly. The life of a garden is ever changing. It may have less obvious splendor in the winter but the soil is indeed active.

Some plants and animals survive during the winter months by going deeper, some by expelling water from their roots, or by creating a sort of antifreeze, or by hibernating. There are organisms that live in symbiotic relationship with one another to cooperatively survive.

Millions of microorganisms stay busy in the winter soil. There is a lot that goes on underground. I could call it riotous ecstasy. Afterall, the duties of roots during the growing season? Transport water and nutrients to everything going on above ground. So yeah, I like to picture the roots down there in the winter - partying a bit.
Amazing.

"Don't think the garden loses its ecstasy in the winter. It's quiet but the roots are down there riotous."

Consciousness can be described as a river or web of energy that goes everywhere. Maybe it **is** luminescent. I imagine *being able to* reach out *and* to

159

mingle with, touch, stretch, stir and connect with its vitality.
Consciousness. Any time. I like that. That's what God is to me. A web of
existence and energy that connects everything.

There is a science to awe and consciousness. In Dacher Keltner's recent
book "Awe, the New Science of Everyday Wonder", he describes
physiological effects of awe and notes that the presence of awe is the
primary indicator of happiness. It transforms the way we think.

Awe - that deep connection with consciousness that can reset the mind,
change our perspective and even quiet our inflammatory response. The
largest bundle of nerves in our body, the Vagus Nerve, slows the
heartbeat, deepens breathing, and regulates digestion and other vital organ
functions. Since awe often happens in nature, Dacher Keltner says "There
is nothing nature can't heal".

Awe is that feeling of being in the presence of something VAST that
transcends our current understanding of the world. It's something we can
barely make sense of and highly emotional.

Things really DO happen when we stop to smell the roses. When we dig in
our gardens and see all that life happening, our nervous system quiets
down. We feel connected to Universal consciousness. We heal. There is
nothing nature can't heal.

> *"Don't think the garden loses its ecstasy in the winter. It's quiet but the*
> *roots are down there riotous."*

Last year one of my garden beds, planted and tended with care, just started to disappear - plant by plant. Yes, gophers. Gophers had breached my chicken wire and other deterrents. I had to "let it go". I surrendered that bed.

Last month Bill moved the bed, reinforced it with metal cloth. I had a teenager to move the soil. But there was a significant gardening step between.

You see, I had simultaneously been clearing out boxes. I was sorting memorabilia. Letters from the 70's when I lived away from home as a 14-year-old - far away - in Australia.

This box held letters to my family, from my family, letters filled with adventures, homesickness, connections. Letters from my father, who died shortly after I returned home. A painful ten-page letter to my friend Jane, written as I sat vigil with Pop.

I read them all.

There were letters from college when I once again lived far from home. This time in Europe - letters filled with adventures, longing, insights and connections. Letters to and from my family and friends. Emotional letters with poetry from a best friend in high school. I was the first person she "came out" to.

An impressive number of friends shared pages and pages of emotion. They shared how much they valued and trusted me. Every one of these letters I read again. Letters from me. To me. There were a lot of letters. I filled more than one waste basket with these memories –

now surrendered.

I was ready to surrender them (After all, I hadn't looked at some of them in 50 years.) But a trash bin didn't feel right. Burn them? Yeah, that might work. But then…

I remembered a practice from before shredders and recycle bins. We would dig holes, bury papers, wet them - soil, paper, water, soil.
So yes, I gave my past a true burial. Layers lined my garden box. 1970's, 80's, 90's now living under the soil. Becoming part of the soil. Relationships, emotions, connections, poetry - all becoming part of the soil.

It seems a poetic justice. I wrote them, read them, stored them, moved with them, read them again, let them go - and in the coming months - years even, they will cycle back to me again in a new form.

I picture the roots of my flowers and vegetables absorbing words, sentiments, poems and pictures along with microorganisms. Feeding the web, the soil of consciousness. The roots down there quiet but riotous.

Awesome Indeed.

163

Belonging
By: Steve Burns

In the summer after high school graduation, I joined my brother on a four-week outdoor adventure with NOLS—an Outdoor Leadership/Survival Training School. This was a chance to spend time with my older brother who had initiated the adventure. At the end of the course was a survival period, where you handed in all your food and were given only the map location for pickup three days and 29 miles later. We drank directly out of the streams in those days and in the Wyoming wilderness that was still safe. Food was whatever you could find or catch.

To begin the survival portion, the course instructors had put the possible leader's names in a hat and drew them out, and asked if that person was willing to lead a small group. My name was the first drawn, and I had been surprised. Though uncertain, I accepted, and knew that my brother pined for this opportunity. (He was not chosen.)

On this day we were traversing a range near the top of the peaks. We had to cross over from one peak to the other, and as we rounded the corner, we could see only a patch of snow connecting the two—and a distance of perhaps 70 yards. We could either make this crossing or trek down the small mountain to the base and then back up the adjacent mountain. Our elevation was at least 800-1000 feet, and after our group of four consulted, I had to make the decision. Now was a moment of truth for us, and I decided to accept the group's preference of crossing the snow bridge.

Out of caution, and not knowing exactly the condition of the snow, we used our rope and tied ourselves together. I went first and crossed slowly, planting each step carefully. Earlier in our course we had practiced 'self-arrest' on a snowfield, and learned how hard it was to stop a full slide when wearing a heavy pack and dragging an ice axe. As soon as I reached the other side, I could see the snowfield clearly from a new vantage point. It was significantly undercut, like a muffin top, with the depth of the snow narrowing toward the thin edge. I hollered to the others still crossing to go higher as they crossed, and could hardly breathe as I watched each of them make their way across. I felt great relief after all were across, and had intermittent dreams (not good ones) of the other outcomes afterwards.

On this course, we learned how to form solid bonds, not only with ropes but of trust and care. Truly each of our lives were in the hands of each other, for it was wilderness and you never knew what might happen next. I savored the time with my brother, traveling in the car to our big adventure and being tent-mates up until survival when we were in different groups.

My concept of belonging has many facets, both personal and spiritual. I have had many unexplainable and improbable experiences. I believe that there is a force in the universe which both creates and supports life and also connects us not only to each other, but also other living beings. On that day, traversing the fragile snowfield, I believe the physics of the forces holding the snow and ice together did not require any metaphysical effects for our safe crossing. And while we may exit this world alone, our journey through life is made richer and much more tolerable if we maintain strong connections with others.

Live with the Questions
By: Elli Norris

"Be patient toward all that is unsolved in your heart and try to love the questions themselves, like locked rooms and like books that are now written in a very foreign tongue. Do not now seek the answers, which cannot be given you because you would not be able to live them. And the point is, to live everything. **Live the questions now.** *Perhaps you will then gradually, without noticing it, live along some distant day into the answer."*

- Rainer Maria Rilke from *Letters to a Young Poet*

In *Letters to a Young Poet,* Rilke was responding to a query from a young officer candidate in military school who was drawn to a literary life, the life of a poet. The young man[11] asked Rilke for his advice. In one of his responses, Rilke said (I paraphrase) "Don't seek the answers… live the questions."

What does Rilke mean? As I've pondered that question these past weeks I've come to many possible "answers." Not to that never-to-be-answered one, "Where does life come from?" No, but answers about how to respond to the questions that come with everyday life.

The one that is most satisfying to me right now comes out of an experience from long ago.

Many years ago, I sat with my sister as she approached her death, much too young, after a year's battle with cancer. Our relationship had not been an easy one—she the big sister nearly five years older than I, and I, the competing (so she thought) "little sister."

But in her illness, circumstances - call it fate? - gave me the chance to sit with her for a few moments while everyone else was out of her room. I pulled my chair up beside her bed and took her hand. She was so small, so frail. She asked me to put a small pillow beneath her head and somehow one hand knew to lift her head as I slipped the pillow under it with the other hand. I stroked her hand gently and we talked quietly about simple things. Not about her illness and what surely we both knew was her approaching death. Just daily stuff. And then the moment ended and it was time for me to leave. But the relationship which had so often been rough had become…smooth.

What was the question here? Did I ask myself what to say or do for my sister? Perhaps… for a fleeting second. What I believe is that something in me had known what was needed. Simply… be present.

I believe this "Something" exists within each one of us and knows that if we live with the question, the answer will come, not only in some distant day as Rilke promises, but in the very moment that we need that one answer.

All we have to do is TRUST in that Something. No small task!

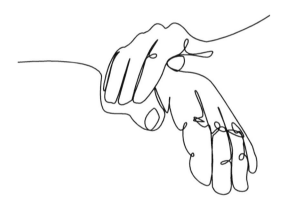

Letting Go
By: Emily Burstein

My youngest child Avery just left home to live with three friends from Mills College. Their house is on Alice Street, right behind Avery's old Junior High. But, you say, isn't Mills College in Oakland? That's correct, but due to the Pandemic, school is online. So anywhere works. Just as an FYI, Avery is ok with me sharing this reflection.

This past March 2020, Avery, who is trans, and uses they/them pronouns, abruptly was sent home from their first year at Mills along with all the other students to finish the semester online. It was lovely to have Avery home again. We ordered a weekly organic vegetable box. Avery cooked us lush meals. I was sous-chef and dishwasher. We watched countless TV series and cooking shows, and burrowed on Avery's bed with our dog, A.J.

But, with no support and camaraderie from dear Mills friends, Avery struggled to hold their depression at bay. We couldn't imagine how Avery could survive the next year of online school at home. Slowly, Avery and three Mills' friends developed a plan to live in Davis for the year while attending school online.

Avery and I were in charge of the hunt, as the others lived elsewhere. Now, a few months later, Avery's bedroom furniture is gone from my house and lives in a welcoming room with bright but gentle light bouncing off sage-colored walls.

But getting there was rough. I wanted so badly for the plan to work and felt so responsible. The kids had a tight budget and wanted a house with a backyard. Avery checked listings. I double-checked them. When we found something promising, I pushed Avery to have the group immediately fill out applications. Almost daily I nagged Avery to talk to their friends.

For a while, with every conversation we had, my pulse raced, and my muscles were so contracted they ached. I would catch the sound of my voice and it was so ugly, I wished it wasn't mine. I felt like a pressure cooker that might explode with half-cooked lentils all over the kitchen.

Slowly, we found our equilibrium. I let myself notice how competent and responsible Avery was skillfully forging a respectful and efficient decision-making process with their friends. I realized I didn't have to or even want to control everything. I could simply support and facilitate.

My worry about Avery lessening, I turned to my own fears. I told myself, Avery may never live at home again. I worried I might need to social distance from Avery and not be able to see them. And, I was absolutely sure I would be left sad, old and alone, with only occasional walks with friends and my dear dog.

But on my first visit to Alice Steet, it was so clear that the kids had already made the house into a home. And they warmly invited me in. I felt the sadness slip off my body and a warm lightness enter.

Back at my own house, I savored a tingling anticipation of change. I moved into Avery's old, larger room, with wonderful south-facing light and the big window filled with sky and leaves. Avery's pine slab Ikea desk made me significantly more organized than my previous desk at the dining room table.

The spare room, with some of its furniture gone to Alice Street, could now fit a long rolled-up Persian rug of my grandparents to cushion my feet in my new home yoga studio.

A week after Avery left, I took my first yoga class in almost two months. I settled into the familiar sound of the teacher's voice as she explained the Sanskrit word *Spanda*. It means a pulsation of the body. Expansion as wide as imagination and contraction, not tense, but like a hug.

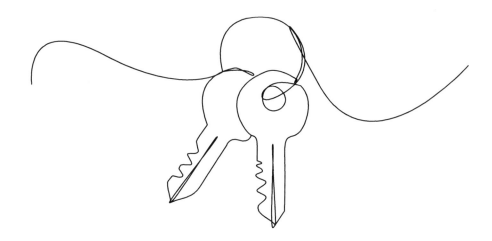

Decision Debt, Integrity and the Toilet Paper Aisle
By: Sarah Larkin

I want to be a person of great integrity - to be honest, respectful, kind, make all of the "right" choices. I would venture to guess that most of us WANT to be honest people with strong ethics and morals, but if you're like me, maybe you get lost in the gray area and don't exactly know what you're doing.

For example, what does a person with integrity do when they've made a commitment, and when commitment time comes, they wish they could go home and take a bubble bath instead? Do they keep their commitment with the outside world or do they honor their commitment to themselves? What is the "right" thing to do. I really don't know. Some folks would say, honoring the external commitment is the obvious choice. Other folks might say, you have to take care of yourself first before you are able to tend to outside commitments.

I often find myself consumed in the confusion that comes from the dualities of the internal and the external. I can get seriously lost in trying to figure out what the "best" or "right" choice is. Sometimes, when I see the stakes as high, I buckle under the pressure. I give up, run away, hide or procrastinate so I don't have to face making a choice. On the other end of the spectrum, there are times that I will make a choice quickly to get it over with. Sometimes it is fun and I feel blessed with an abundance of choices, and sometimes I feel stifled and desperately seek direction, limits and clarity.

As adults, we make around 35,000 conscious decisions every day. It must be true because google said so. I didn't realize the enormity and complexity of the decision making process, and I got myself into decision debt. Decision debt is what occurs when I file decisions away for later because I am locked into such a state of fear and confusion that I can't make a decision. Sometimes after I file a decision away, it becomes obsolete and I never have to make the decision...most times they just join the pile. But the thing is, with 35,000 decisions daily, the pile can get out of control so fast, and I drag it with me everywhere I go. Its presence can be daunting and oppressive and leads to more fear and scarcity.

No wonder I used to get overwhelmed in the toilet paper aisle! Has that ever happened to you? One ply, two ply, mega rolls, super mega rolls, forest friendly, on sale, cute cuddly bear, angel, or puppy? I'm trying to sort through all of the options with my huge pile of indecisions falling all over the place waiting impatiently. HANG ON! I'm trying to pick toilet paper right now! Not only would I get overwhelmed in the toilet paper aisle, I would then shame and berate myself for being so incompetent that I couldn't handle picking out toilet paper. You know what doesn't help you feel like a competent adult? Shaming and berating yourself over toilet paper. You don't even want to know how much energy has been spent on toilet paper drama. And what about the other 34,999 choices waiting to be made AFTER I figure out the toilet paper situation? It is exhausting.

I have a plan to address this decision debt situation I find myself in and get it cleaned up. I'd love to share it with you in case you have your own debt you'd like to address.

Step 1. Recognize how many decisions I am faced with every day. Doing this allows me to hold perspective. Toilet paper no longer makes the 35,000 cut. I get the same kind of toilet paper at Costco. Every. Single.

178

Time. Put it in the cart, and let's go. It is now in auto-pilot mode. Next!

Step 2. Giving myself permission to not make the perfect choice every time. The law of averages is on my side. Even if 3,500 of the 35,000 choices I make aren't perfect, I still have an A average. That's good enough for me.

Step 3. Giving myself permission to make a different choice. This eases the burden to know that if this choice doesn't work out, I can pick something different. Bye-bye drama.

Step 4. Toss shame in the garbage. Seriously. It's not welcome anymore.

Step 5. Become clearer with myself so that I can be clear with others. Clear communication is kind communication.

For me, growing fully into a life led with integrity starts with getting out of decision debt and cultivating clarity within my own mind so that I have a strong base from which I can make decisions quickly, easily and kindly. Once I have that foundation set, I will be free to explore what extra layers of integrity I want to add into my life. I invite us all to look at our foundations with fresh eyes. Does it need some attention so that we may build great things upon it?

Shaken to My Bones
By: Donna Sachs

I am one of the people who is a part of the Beloved Conversations program. We are being invited to reflect in many ways—on our church, our society and ourselves.

One theme has been to explore our whiteness. Is this part of our identity? Do I even have to think about it? What about white privilege? I reflected, and I recalled an experience when my sense of privilege was shattered in a way that was truly terrifying.

I grew up with a sense that respect was a human right that should be extended to everyone. I came to understand that the world contained much injustice, but I held to my ideals and my own rather narrow experience. I was used to being treating with respect by others.

Then one day when I was a university student in Ann Arbor, Michigan, I had a car accident. I was driving through the city in the midst of a deluge of a rainstorm. A car suddenly stopped ahead of me and I rear-ended it. A minor accident. No one hurt. The police came and I was given a ticket. Not just a ticket, but a summons to appear in court.

So I went to court and had to present my case. The judge barely listened and set a fine that was surprisingly large. Then, I was told by the bailiff to go stand in line at a certain window. So I did. A long line. When I reached the window, the man took my papers and said to give him the money. Well, I had not brought my checkbook and I certainly did not have enough money in my wallet to pay this fine. He barely looked at me, his manner was disinterested and his eyes were cold. He said, "If you can't pay, you go to jail". I said, "I can pay, but I do not have it with me. My bank is just down the street". He said, "You have to pay now. Please step aside." and gestured over to the bailiff. The line was long and I could feel impatience behind me. I was stunned and did not know what to do so I just stayed standing there in front of him. Then he said, "Ok, go get your money."

This was in the late 1960's when much social unrest and protest were happening in Ann Arbor and Detroit. I learned that the Ann Arbor police were being especially hard on students during that time.

As for me, on that day I was shaken to my bones. The lack of respect floored me. And what if I had not had enough money? Would they really have put me in jail? I remember I walked out of that court thinking, "So this is what it is like to be poor. This is what can happen if you are poor."

When the Sacred Shatters
By: Kirk Ridgeway

The theme of today's service is "When the Sacred Shatters." On reading this title, my very first question was "What is sacred?"

If I were a monotheistic fundamentalist zealot, the answer would be easy. I would simply say something like God, Allah, Jehovah or some other deified name. But I am of the Unitarian Universalist persuasion. How do I answer this? If, as we say, everything is interdependent then everything is sacred. And if everything is sacred then what do I worship? Where do I go for sanctuary? What can I hold onto in the chaos of this world?

Taking this a step further, if everything is sacred then what do we mean when we add the word "sacred," as an adjective, to describe "this" as being "sacred" and "that" as being profane? What makes this place "sacred" and not Peet's or Taco Bell. Does our chalice cease to be sacred when we blow out the candle and store it in the closet? Are sacred vows nothing but hollow words? All these questions, leading to more questions, a Pandora's Box of questions, each time I come up with "the answer" to "What is Sacred?"

In researching this question, I found that the roots of the word "sacred" include the early Roman religious word "*sacer*" which meant anything "set apart" from common society...that is, anything set apart from the commonplace activities of everyday life. In Roman temple architecture, it meant the interior of a pagan temple where visitors needed to be attentive to the needs of the gods.

As I thought about this, I reflected on years ago, living in Pleasanton, where there was a small park that contained a decaying art sculpture made of metal and wood. Weeds were gradually engulfing it. I would go there to sit on an equally dilapidated bench. It was a quiet place for me, a meditative space, a space where I could focus my attention and at times enter a state of awe and reverence. It became a sacred place for me where I stepped away from my everyday habituated activities and thoughts. One day I arrived at the park and found that the statue had been bulldozed down. Though I knew it was only metal and wood, that it was rusted and rotten, its disappearance created a hole in my chest. My sacred place was shattered.

There have been other sacred shatterings in my life. Shattered objects, shattered beliefs, shattered relationships and still the experience of sacredness survives and deepens my question as to "What is sacred?"

What I can only say for now is that for me, certain objects, places, and relationships are sacred - that the Great Mystery of life is sacred. That sacredness is a confluence, a matrix of conditions, a flow of interactions, a dynamic process that evokes attention to what is worthy, to what illuminates the ultimate concerns of life. "What is sacred" is that which we value as touchstones of love and awareness that unite the shattered pieces of life.

186

I applied to be a Worship Associate at the end of my term as finance officer for UUCD. I wanted to get to know people on a different level, one that would round out my relationship with the congregation from the budget presenter to one that asks thought-provoking questions, recalling memories of joy and hardship, and as a storyteller. Storytelling is a uniquely human superpower; no other animal tells stories the way humans do – for meaning-making and relationship building.

Stacie Hartung Frerichs

The Wisdom of Generosity
By: Stanley Dawson

I visited the Ranch near Fresno every year for the month of August from age eight. The first time was on the train with my mother. The next year I went on the train by myself from Palo Alto to Fresno station through the lush green of the Nile Valley and then the bare flat San Joaquin Valley. Granddad met me and drove me the dozen or so miles south on US 99 to the Ranch. That year I started picking grapes for him and his crew of Oakies at 3½ cents per 22 pounds on a tray, finally rising to 5 cents with his Mexican crew during the war.

After that trip, I was allowed to take the bus south on US 101 from San Jose to Gilroy, then another bus towards the east, pausing for delightful ice cream after the bus made its first big climb out of Gilroy. Then over Pacheco Pass to Madera and finally another bus south on US 99 to be let off at the Ranch, as marked by a restaurant with an airplane sticking up out of the building's roof.

I admired the scenic wonder of Pacheco Pass. I even started to memorize the statuesque look of the oaks on those golden rolling hills and to keep my eyes up for redtail hawks. It brings to mind Kate Wolf's later poetic rendering of the song about the Golden Rolling Hills of California. It starts:

> *"Driving all day up the San Joaquin*
> *Turn west again up through Pacheco.*
> *Through the blue hills back of Santa Cruz*
> *Where the red tail hawks go circling*
> *Like the ways of time."*

189

During college times, I still visited the Ranch in summers. So I got to drive myself over Pacheco several times in my flashy red 1937 Chevy Coup, to visit those generous Grandparents who had been so splendid to me. Grandma was actually a fundamentalist Christian, and her generosity extended to me in accepting my atheism, only saying that going to church was good, even for nonbelievers, especially going with grandparents.

Her generosity finally seemed to be passed on to me in one trip over Pacheco that turned out to be a special adventure. At the approach to the Pacheco Pass from Gilroy on the West, I saw a hitchhiker and stopped to pick him up. He was very grateful in a gentle way – good company. As we descended from the glories of Pacheco, we came across a car with a flat tire beside the road with the driver signaling for help. After I checked his situation, I thought it best to take him to get a new tire in the little town at the bottom of the long grade. I took him down and back and he gave me perhaps $20, which I took, being a student. But then I thought, "Here is an opportunity to give my hitchhiking passenger some money," so I convinced my passenger to take half the money back on the grounds that I liked to share. The good feeling I got from that made me a more generous person for much of the rest of my life.

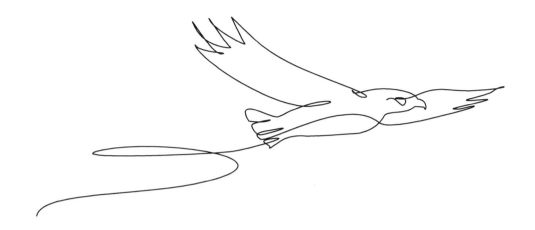

I've Looked at "Mom" from Both Sides Now
By: Carlena Wike

Truth is not subject to schedule –

Not beholden to demand,

And feels no obligation.

Still, when we pause,

suspend belief

And wait

Truth will loosen one more veil,

And strike us dumb with our unknowing…

It is then the heart has ears.

~ Carlena Wike

My mother was beautiful, intelligent, witty, strong willed and outspoken. She roared into the 1920s, did a two-fisted celebration of Prohibition, and in 1935 married her third husband, John Rolfe Pratt, my father.

My struggles as a child born to a non-stereotypical mother turned out to be very valuable--almost as valuable as my subsequent struggle to live up to the expectations I placed upon myself as a mother.

I believe my parents were deeply in love when they married, but it is not a part of their relationship I remember. The marriage seemed to veer off track in 1942 when my father enlisted in the army, leaving my mother at home with five children and little money.

Mother felt betrayed. As she put it, "John waltzed off in a wave of patriotism; at thirty-nine years of age and with five children at home, he did not have to serve at all."

My father, a trauma surgeon, was with the first wave of American troops to hit Normandy Beach. He came home with shrapnel wounds and what was then called "shell shock." Mother said "the man who returned from the war was not the man I married." Their marriage never recovered and the home I remember was a war zone.

I am reminded of the dysfunction in my family as I follow today's news of soldiers who come home suffering from post-traumatic stress disorder and try to reintegrate into the families they left. I think of their children.

My first marriage, at the age of nineteen, was a grab for stability. I deliberately chose a man who did not drink and who had already served in the military. Determined to create the type of home I'd idealized in the Dick and Jane early readers, I set out to be the kind of mother I felt mine had not been. After fourteen years, two children, and three years of therapy, I chose single motherhood over my two-parent travesty and moved on.

I was a fierce mother, determined not to inflict the wounds of my childhood on my children. I prepared hot breakfasts, reminded the children to take their sweaters, brush their teeth, look before crossing and respect their teachers. I volunteered at their schools, was an Indian Maiden, a Tai Kwan Do mom, drove them to swim classes, music lessons and introduced them to soccer, baseball and Ron Wike.

Ron and I met at Emerson Unitarian Church in Canoga Park. We fell in love and were married there three years later. We sold our homes and purchased a house on horse property so that Gigi could have a horse and Jon could roam the Simi hills.

Somewhere in the middle of high school, Gigi declared herself emancipated, took me to task and informed me that as a mother, I had not measured up to her expectations. I wanted to defend myself, fight the charges and scream, but something, (and here I'll call it God's hand), bade me listen. I heard her out, managed to remain civil and made a hasty retreat. My daughter was telling me I had failed her as a mother. My deepest fear had been confirmed.

I learned that gifts are often found in hard places, but it took time and quite a bit of wound licking before I was able to unwrap this one. My eventual insight and acceptance proved life changing. Acknowledging that my daughter's perceptions represented her truth and that her pain would be better addressed in the therapist's office rather than in a round of accusations and denials between the two of us, I was able to celebrate her wisdom in seeking help.

Realizing the impossibility of changing the past, I agonized over what I might possibly have to offer the situation. "I am still her mother," I reminded myself. "What does a grown woman need from her mother?" I decided to let Gigi guide our relationship.

This experience led to a softening of the anger I held against my mother. I wondered what judgements she had harbored against her mother and I forgave her — something I had not thought possible.

195

My mother gave me life. The window into this world for anyone of us is narrow and the odds are against us — A few fertile hours, a single ovum, a single sperm, one woman, one man. My mother was in love with my father when that window opened for me and I was singled out for life.

I did the same for my daughter. I gave her life. Now I must let her live it.

Emergence
By: Lorraine Nail Visher

Where are you walking now?
I imagine the smell of snow.
You reached over to pat your dog,
your back turned to us,
creating a private moment,
moving away.
I understand the fear
that a photograph
might capture your soul.

The years of sacrificing yourself
for us — and for others
has sufficed.
From your childhood cocoon
   of bitterness and distrust
you twisted the strands and re-wove a life
of incredible beauty.
And although your gifts
did not always fall
where I judged they were needed most,
it is significant that they fell at all.

Pixie dust to Senior Ball gowns.
PTA Carnivals to funding for day care.
You believed in the power of magic
as fiercely as you denied
the power of evil.

Failure was not an option.
Self-aggrandizement
Was not your goal.

I walk in the sun now.
It rarely snows here.
The most we can hope for is frost.
A sunflower pinned against a wire fence
presses its face towards me.
I think of you reaching outward
   all your life,
beyond the curtain of pain
that descended round your bed at birth.
The courage to reach…
even if you could not walk through.

I do not pick the blossom.
Days later, someone else does.
It does not matter.
I feel you lingering,
outside the door of the church,
watching me sing.
I catch you peering at me sideways
from the eyes of magpies.

Slowly I release you from my veins.
You turn into vapor.
Blending into a remembered snowfall.
Turning away from me.
Reappearing at a distance.

Leaning
Into the sunshine
I wait.

My mother[12] never used the word social justice; she simply lived it by starting a day care program for disadvantaged families, providing a safe and healthy environment for their children. She never knew how her work might have changed the lives of the parents and children involved, but there is little doubt that it did. Years later that program was dismantled by a board of directors that falsely accused her of graft because she loaned money from her own checking account to meet payroll when the state budget stalled. Although this saddened her, I know she never regretted those years.

Margret was an adult child of an alcoholic father, who was lost to her when her parents bitterly divorced. My mother continually gave herself away, first to my siblings and to me, later to her daycare program and to other lost children. As a child, I resented that. When a woman is pregnant we say she is "expecting". Now I wonder what did my mother expect from her own life and actions? Were her dreams larger than the selfish childhood expectations I held for her? The gifts parents give are not always to their children but to a greater hope beyond their children.

To give birth to a child, a dream, or simply another morning takes great courage and we rarely get to see the results of that effort. My mother didn't live long enough to see the mature teacher I have become and she will never know the dynamic people I believe her granddaughters are growing to be. But she surely reached out, laying a hand on me and, through me, to them. As I release my adult daughters into their own lives, I realize I am doing the same.

Leaning
Into the sunshine
I wait.

199

200

Notes

How Unitarian Universalism's Six Sources are Performing in the Climate Crisis: Robin Datel

The six sources of Unitarian Universalism (https://www.uua.org/beliefs/what-we-believe/sources, accessed January 10, 2024)

[1] Direct experience of that transcending mystery and wonder, affirmed in all cultures, which moves us to a renewal of the spirit and an openness to the forces which create and uphold life;

[2] Words and deeds of prophetic people which challenge us to confront powers and structures of evil with justice, compassion, and the transforming power of love;

[3] Wisdom from the world's religions which inspires us in our ethical and spiritual life;

[4] Jewish and Christian teachings which call us to respond to God's love by loving our neighbors as ourselves;

[5] Humanist teachings which counsel us to heed the guidance of reason and the results of science, and warn us against idolatries of the mind and spirit;

[6] Spiritual teachings of Earth-centered traditions which celebrate the sacred circle of life and instruct us to live in harmony with the rhythms of nature.

[*] Tending and Gathering Garden is located at the Cache Creek Nature Preserve, Yolo County, California. CacheCreekConservancy.org

A Sacred Covenant of Unconditional Love, Respect and Trust: Lily Roberts

[7] Excerpt from the UUCD Covenant.

Notes

A Lily Among Roses: Lily Roberts

[8] Brief History of the Flower Communion:

    The creator of the Flower Communion, Norbert Capek, said *"Religion should, before all else, provide that "inner harmony which is the precondition of strong character, good health, joyful moods and victorious, creative life."* His words helped me remember the inner peace and joy I felt when I was five - lying on the ground with my friend, feeling safe inside the big, blue bubble. Imagine, if you will, a "teddy bear" that is always there when you need a hug – that is a feeling of inner harmony.

    I am also reminded how important it has been over the years to be able to connect to that inner harmony through time in nature, or meditation, or sharing special time with friends and family. We cannot be creative, healthy, joyous, or victorious if we are not able to feel safe and be at peace.

    Dr. Capek was very creative in his life. Not only did he create the flower communion almost 100 years ago, but he also wrote over 90 hymns. Some are in our hymnal, like "Mother Spirit, Father Spirit" and "Color of Fragrance." He also started a religious school and a Unitarian Church in Prague, Czechoslovakia, that grew to be the largest congregation in the world by 1941. Sadly, Dr. Capek and his daughter were arrested that year, and later, he was killed by the Nazis. His legacy continues today because the flower communion takes place each year in UU congregations all over the world.

    The flower communion honors each individual's contribution to the community, while signifying the importance of community that supports enduring and meaningful relationships. We have Norbert Capek and his wife, Maja, to thank for this wonderful tradition. His life's work and sacrifice is honored as we celebrate the flower communion each spring. Let us say *muchas gracias* - many thanks!

Notes

The Importance of Collective Action: Marty West

[9] Originally written September 4, 2011, as a Labor Day Life Journey

Wisdom of Crows: Susan Steinbach

[10] Intern Minister Kate Kennedy gave me this prompt: "What I'd like you to be thinking about for your Call to Worship is your experience of nature - your connection to the earth - perhaps a profound moment. Experiment with writing from a different perspective."

Growing Up Catholic: Stacie Frerichs

Being a Worship Associate prompted me to dive deeply into my religious history growing up as Catholic, serving as one of the first altar girls in my Los Angeles parish or going to Catholic mass lead by Pope John Paul II at Dodger Stadium with my mom while I was still in elementary school. My reflection on belief and doubt delves into the questions we ask as UUs about our values and guiding philosophy.

Live with the Questions: Elli Norris

[11] Franz Xaver Kappus, Wikipedia

Emergence: Lorraine Nail Visher

[12] Mother's Day can be a difficult day for me. My mother died on May 7, 1999, two days before Mother's Day. I wrote the poem Emergence for her 4 months after she died. I shared it in this reflection on Mother's Day almost ten years later.

203

Notes

Cover Art: Catlyn LeGault

The flaming chalice is a symbol of the Unitarian Universalist tradition that has roots going back to WWII when the Unitarian Service Committee used it on documents assisting Jewish refugees escape Nazi persecution. Over time, the symbol has evolved in scope, meaning, and style.

Adding her own personal touch, church member and artist Peg Rutger created a one-of-a-kind stained-glass chalice for the Unitarian Universalist Church of Davis (UUCD). The flame in her depiction is a phoenix and through the glass, the flames of the phoenix are lit by the sun. Since its creation, it has hung at the front of UUCD's sanctuary, a centerpiece for worship and a unique symbol for our church.

The Title

Our group of five met regularly over Zoom to collaborate on this project, always opening with some words of inspiration and by lighting a chalice to set our intentions. After Lorraine read this poem during one of our chalice lightings, the book's title became instantly illuminated from her words: *The Outline of Our Souls*. Our months-long search for a title was complete.

Donors

Thank you to these angels, who generously donated $50 or more to help jumpstart this project:

Robert Bakke & Lily Roberts

Emily Burnstein

Carol Corbett

Robin Datel

Robert J. Dowling & Susan Steinbach

Sharon Hale & Dawn M.M. Student

Charles Halsted & Ann Halsted

Grady Hesters & Linda Olsen

Jeannette Hogan

Susan Jellema

Karen Klussendorf Kurth & William Kurth

Mary Higgins MacDonnell

Anne McKeever

Karen Naliboff

Elli Norris

Jill Pickett

Kirk Ridgeway & Linda Ridgeway

Don Saylor & Julie Saylor

Claudia Utts-Smith

Lorraine Nail Visher

Marty West

Also, a thank you to all the others who gave their money, time, and talent to help out.

207

Made in the USA
Columbia, SC
22 October 2024

44620532R00122